RISE UP

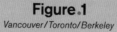

Figure.1
Vancouver / Toronto / Berkeley

LEADERSHIP HABITS FOR TURBULENT TIMES

ALI GROVUE & MIKE WATSON

22 23 24 25 26   5 4 3 2

Cataloguing data is available from Library and Archives Canada
ISBN 978-1-77327-176-7 (hbk.)
ISBN 978-1-77327-177-4 (ebook)
ISBN 978-1-77327-178-1 (pdf)

Design by Naomi MacDougall
Illustration by bulentgultek/iStock
Authors' photographs by Jamie Boyce

Editing by Steve Cameron
Copy editing by Judy Phillips
Proofreading by Alison Strobel
Indexing by Stephen Ullstrom

Printed and bound in Canada by Friesens
Distributed internationally by Publishers Group West

Some names and identifying details have been changed to protect the privacy of individuals.

Figure 1 Publishing Inc.
Vancouver BC Canada
www.figure1publishing.com

Contents

PREFACE

MIKE WATSON

AM A fortunate person. The work I do for a living—leading Ignite Management Services in its mission to facilitate strategy and leadership development for individuals and teams—is deeply linked to my passion and purpose. It has not been easy getting to this point. There were times in my life and career where it would appear I had it all—a great family, a position of influence, good health, and good friends. Yet I was unfulfilled. In hindsight, it is easy to see that I thought I was a good leader but wasn't. I thought that I had all the answers but didn't. It was a lack of meaningful connection with those I worked with that left me unfulfilled.

I spent a lot of time in my career being a bottom line-focused leader who generated great fiscal results, often at the expense of the well-being of the people I worked with. It took me decades to realize that being a great leader isn't about building clever strategy, enhancing shareholder wealth, or charting top-quartile performance. No, being a great leader is about enabling people, individually and collectively, to be the best versions of themselves in pursuit of noble goals.

Reflecting on my career, I realize that there were many moments—unfortunately—where I was blind to the cost of my leadership style that put profit over people. One moment in particular stands out. In my thirties, I was an executive in a midsized financial services firm. I was tasked to build and execute a new strategy to make the firm more relevant to the clients we served and aspired to serve. Regrettably, I had already done a poor job of building trust with my executive colleagues—well, that's a small understatement. Nevertheless, I was given the opportunity. The goal was to transform the institution from one that was transactional to one that was predicated on interaction and advice.

This project was not for the faint of heart. Institutional behaviors and systems supporting a transactional environment were culturally embedded. Yet, shifting our focus was the right thing to do. Banking was becoming commoditized; we needed a strategy that would combat this trend. Our firm needed to shift our activities from centering on the products we sold to centering on the advice we provided.

After completing significant research, I put pen to paper and crafted a vision, strategy, and tactical framework that would ensure successful implementation of the firm's plan. This was not to be a small change. In fact, it would be transformational. So much so that it required the board's approval. Imagine my ego when I presented the strategy to the board members and they applauded and agreed to fully fund it. I felt like I could conquer the world.

I took the approval to my senior leadership team to begin implementation. I told them what we needed to start doing and what we needed to stop doing. It was a road map that would lead us all to remarkable success! I was on fire, and this was to be my greatest career triumph. However, I would soon learn one of the most important lessons of my life: Wisdom doesn't grow on our good days.

Once we launched, I watched our results drop. Not just a little. Our results dropped in every conceivable category: customer engagement, financial margins, and employee engagement. Month after month I waited with bated breath for the turnaround. But it didn't happen. Before the launch, I understood that some of the changes would not be popular, and I was prepared to fight for them. But I was not prepared for this. Six months in, my great triumph was on the path to being a spectacular disaster. I was devastated and I finally broke down. In a rare moment of humility, I went to the office of a trusted colleague, closed the door, and let it all out.

"What," I asked, "is happening? Why don't they get it?"

With a caring look and a hint of a smile, my colleague said, "Come on, Mike. You know."

"I don't know," I said, fuming. "What the hell is going on?"

"You really want to know?" she asked.

"Yes, damnit! I want to know!"

"Mike," she quietly explained, "employees don't like you. You came in here like a bull in a china shop. You came in here telling people what to do. You have shown no interest in them as people, and you haven't once asked for their input. You have been deeply disrespectful to them."

"And," she continued, "even those who want to buy in are discouraged. When they come to you with suggestions, you are dismissive and tell them why your way is right."

In my life I had never been confronted with such brutal, honest, and accurate feedback. I wept. What she said made perfect sense. It was embarrassing, it was humbling, and, with the problem defined, it was solvable.

This trusted colleague recommended I undertake two tasks.

The first proved to be one of the most challenging of my career. I was instructed to buy a box of doughnuts, deliver them to one of our offices that was particularly troubled, and sit in the lunchroom from 11 a.m. to 2 p.m. There I was to engage with each person who entered the room. I was to ask questions about them and talk about anything but work. It was the toughest three hours of my career to date. I had lost my ability to connect with people.

But it worked. I was shocked by how receptive the employees were to this gesture. Not only did I learn a little bit about their families and their interests, but I also heard about their hopes and dreams. And, with that, the connections started to form.

My second task involved bringing the leadership team together to reboot. I spoke slowly and clearly and apologized for my behavior and approach. And, symbolically, I stood in front of the room, my beloved strategy in hand, and I ripped it in half. I'll never forget that moment. A voice came from the back of the room. It belonged to one of our managers. "Mikey, Mikey," he said. "It's not that bad. We just need to tweak it a little." That day, the team took ownership of the strategy.

Thirteen years later I was thumbing through the business section of a national newspaper and stumbled upon a story of this same organization. I had left a decade ago by then, and it was now being recognized nationally for its vision and strategy. It had exceptional staff engagement, customer loyalty, and financial results. The team owned these results.

The moral of this story is that you cannot have success without trust, and you cannot have trust without engaging people at an individual level. And, for people to engage, they must be invited to share their beliefs, and their goodwill must be accepted as a gift.

WHILE THE JOURNEY of writing this book started years ago, clarity on why it mattered came to me only recently, when my mother-in-law passed away. This began the laborious process of my father-in-law cleaning out the family home and preparing it for sale as he transitioned into more suitable accommodation. Occasionally, I was conscripted to help. One of my tasks was to go through the papers in his office to differentiate confidential recycling from general recycling. My father-in-law, by then retired, was an accomplished engineer and former business executive, and he had kept every document that had crossed his desk since 1965. With delight—but slowing down the process—I scoured his collection of books and manuals, which referenced many leadership programs.

That is when it hit me. Not much has changed. Leadership continues to be about enhancing the ability of people to be at their best in pursuit of a common goal. His manuals predated famous minds like Peter Drucker, Jim Collins, Patrick Lencioni, and countless others who have written defining books on leadership. And yet, many of the core tenets were the same.

I was deep in the process of research for this book, and, in this moment, it felt like another management book was unnecessary. Why not reexamine the books that have already been written? There are some great ones out there.

Yet, despite the countless books written on the subject and hundreds of millions of dollars invested in the pursuit of enhancing leadership, it seems to me that great leadership remains elusive, when it should have been improving generation to generation.

I believe the reason we are still struggling with consistently providing great leadership to our charges is because understanding the habits that make for a resilient leader is a good start, but it is not enough. Too often at Ignite we see leaders who spend hours contemplating how others need to change but do not look in the mirror and accept that change needs to start with them. What we have learned at Ignite is that the leadership gap is less about the knowledge of what leadership is than it is about the ability to look in the mirror and say:

- I am not a great leader.
- I want to be a great leader.
- I am clear on my motivation to be a better leader.

This is the essence of Ignite's system of leadership development. It is not enough to know what good leadership is. It is not enough to recognize good leadership when we see it. Instead, we need to let go of ego, look in the mirror, and say to ourselves, "I am not a great leader." And we need the desire, rooted in purpose, to be a great leader.

When working with emerging leaders, we ask why they want to invest in leadership development. Their answer to this question helps us understand their motivation. The response is often not direct. But, with a bit of probing, the truth emerges— and far too often the reason is the wrong one: "I want the next promotion."

If this is your motivation, put down this book. It is not for you. Our methodology won't work for you. You might fake it enough to get that next job. But you will get it because you faked it, not because you are a great leader.

If you are ready to be a great leader because of the impact you will have on the well-being of the people in your sphere, *Rise Up* is the book for you. This book will enable you to embrace the attributes of a resilient leader, and it will help you create an environment for your team that allows them to thrive. In order to do so, you are going to have to look deep inside yourself.

For those who struggle with motivation, consider picking up Viktor Frankl's *Man's Search for Meaning* or Clay Christensen's *How Will You Measure Your Life?* and begin a journey of self-discovery. Both books encourage the reader to dig deeper in the pursuit of happiness. Frankl helps readers identify a purpose in life that we will feel positive about while imagining that outcome, and Christensen provides lessons in how to do that by identifying your values and learning to live by them.

This reminds me of an old parable.

The gods had been angered by humankind. They had seen humans squander their gift of divinity through complacency and discontent. The gods decided that they needed to take away humankind's divine power.

"Where shall we hide it?" said one god.

"Let's hide it on the highest mountain," another responded.

"No. Humans are industrious; they will climb the highest mountain in pursuit."

"Perhaps at the bottom of the ocean?" said another god.

"No. Humans are ambitious. They will dive deeper and deeper until they find it."

Finally, it was decided when a god said "I know!" and decreed: "We will hide it inside them; they will never think to look there."

And so it is. Greatness resides inside all of us. But are we willing to do the soul searching and embrace the discomfort necessary to find it?

You can be a great leader. You can inspire people to do things they never felt they could. You can give them hope and belief in themselves. You can help them believe in a vision. You can help them be better teammates. Ultimately, you can create an environment that allows them to soar.

And when you take the time to lift others up, you also lift up yourself. The rewards of great leadership endure on a level far greater than that of individual accolades and success.

Helping people be the best version of themselves is the highest calling of a great leader.

INTRODUCTION

THIS BOOK will help you be a better leader—a leader capable of creating resilient teams and organizations, and a leader who inspires people to be the best version of themselves in pursuit of a common goal. What follows, however, is not a how-to book or instruction manual. If only it were that easy. Instead, this book is intended to help you understand and recognize the six distinct yet deeply interconnected habits of *resilient* leaders. These habits—Trust, Inquisitiveness, Humility, Optimism, Courage, and Discipline—are brought to life in this text through real-life examples taken from our work on the ground as strategic leadership advisers. You will read about people who embody the habits, as well as those who have fallen short of making the right behaviors habitual. These stories are combined with ideas and knowledge derived from academic and psychological research to provide a balance of theory and real-life practice that will enable those who care about leadership to translate the habits into personal action for themselves.

1

My interest in leadership came through personal development. Twenty years ago, as a young person embarking on postsecondary life, I intuited something that it took the next twenty years to understand: we all crave purpose. And it is the journey of personal development—stretching, growing, discovering our gifts and using them to create value and positively impact others—that helps us discover our purpose and generates personal satisfaction and fulfillment. It is through this journey of being the best we can be that we in turn inspire others to be the best they can be. And that, I've learned, is leadership.

Several years before I started working with my coauthor, Mike, I worked as a small-business consultant, helping leaders enhance the strategic and operational functioning of their organizations. I focused on developing and implementing strategy, structure, systems, and processes. While my assistance helped those companies, the experience often left me feeling frustrated; I hadn't found a way to channel the energy of the leaders involved and turn it into sustainable, meaningful change that was leader-led and cascaded down to the people in those organizations.

I was given a master class in leadership in the navy. As an officer, I got a firsthand look at resilient leadership in action. I was able to connect this to my values of personal development and learned how teams are formed and managed. I was fortunate to reconnect with Mike during this time, and we have been working together since to help executives develop capabilities to transform themselves and their organizations through resilient leadership.

We believe that most people are good and want to do good if given the chance. We believe that leadership drives culture, and culture enables strategy. We believe that every leader has the potential to inspire and motivate people to be better versions of themselves. And we have seen firsthand, repeatedly, the impact of leadership on organizational performance.

Our methodology at Ignite Management is built on the premise that there is untapped potential in most organizations, and the gap in actualizing that potential is in strategy and leadership. When we partner with executives, our aim is to facilitate the creation of strategy from within—that is, strategy that is developed and owned by the people in the organization—and to develop leaders who choose to pursue both personal aspirations and strategic business outcomes. Organizations, at their heart, are collections of people, and our work is designed to help those people realize their potential and work together to create positive change.

This book is divided into eight chapters. The first focuses on the concept of resilient leadership: what it is and why it matters. The second discusses the critical importance of having a strong motivating purpose underpinning the desire to grow as a leader. Chapters 3 through 8 explore each of the six habits of resilient leaders in turn. These chapters are based on a central belief: the habits of resilient leaders can be developed by anyone if they are fully embraced and understood, and if the person looking to develop them is motivated to do so through and for others.

The six habits embodied by resilient leaders are intentionally simple and, we hope, relatable. They are habits we strive for in ourselves and that we see in action in the leaders we work with. That doesn't mean, however, that developing them is easy or quick. But it *is* possible. We see that every day.

ONE

RESILIENT LEADERSHIP

MIKE

It is not the strongest of a species that survives,
nor the most intelligent that survives.
It is the one that is most adaptable to change.

CHARLES DARWIN

RENOWNED FUTURIST Gerd Leonhard refers to the twenty-first century as the most transformational time in human history.[1] The corporate world is in a period of perpetual disruption, punctuated by moments of crisis. Around the hallways of businesses worldwide, Darwin's words resonate as never before.

In these transformational times, leaders are called upon to think and act differently. Resilience—the ability to recover from, or adjust easily to, misfortune or change—is the hallmark of great leadership in the twenty-first century. So, why aren't more leaders and more organizations resilient?

The answer to the question above is quite clear: not enough leaders have embraced the goals of a resilient leader. Through our decades of supporting companies, we have learned and accepted one universal truth: The behavior of leaders is the most important factor in determining an organization's ability to adapt. Whether in times of crisis or calm, the following goals should always be the guideposts for any leader and organization:

- Enable individual and collective ability to be inquisitive; understand the impact a changing landscape might have on the organization and its people.

- Create a deliberate and calm environment in which to create and evaluate options and establish the most appropriate path forward.

- Establish individual and collective courage to make the difficult decisions.

- Enable the collective will to persevere.

- Most importantly, enable people, individually and collectively, to be the best versions of themselves in pursuit of a common goal.

How important is adaptability as a pursuit?

In 2010, *Harvard Business Review* shared the results of a study that tracked 4,700 companies and their responses to three previous global recessions. The results are startling. Seventeen percent of the companies didn't survive. Three years later, 80 percent had not regained prerecession growth and profitability, 40 percent hadn't returned to absolute prerecession profitability, and only 9 percent did better in financial metrics postrecession.[2]

This study creates a compelling case for the need for a new approach to organizational resilience.

While the goals outlined above give you the guideposts for resiliency, they don't answer the question of how leaders establish these practices. What we have learned at Ignite is that what you do as a leader to prepare for disruption is far more important than what you do in the face of disruption. And this begins at an individual level with *you* and your ability to embrace these four steps:

- Accept the need to change.
- Develop a purpose-driven motivation to change.
- Learn and apply the habits of resilient leaders.
- Install habitual practices, and develop a personal setback strategy.

Change

Creating a compelling case for change is rarely a difficult task. Whether we are in a relationship that isn't working, are out of shape and struggling to climb a flight of stairs, or are dismayed by the reading of the weight scale we're standing on, the message will be clear. We need to change something. It is no different with leadership. The signals will be clear and will show up in many ways. Dysfunctional teams, subpar business results, and high turnover are just a few examples of indicators that leadership needs to change. But just like with ingrained patterns, the need to change does not always equal the willingness to change. Having the willingness to change is the first step in the challenging process of becoming a resilient leader.

Motivation

Fitness clubs tend to be very busy in January. The post-Christmas rush has many people demonstrating a willingness to change.

They show up at the gym with the best of intentions. Yet, by mid-February, gym attendance is generally back to traditional levels. Many of the people who were willing to change in January quickly run out of steam.

Change is difficult. And, in our experience, if there is not a strong underlying motivation for the change, it will be short-lived.

This holds true in the pursuit of resilient leadership. Willingness to change leadership behavior is not enough. You need a strong underlying motivation to give you the fortitude to stick with it.

Habits of Resilient Leaders

A Google search of the term "leadership" generates over three billion results. Lack of relevant content is not the problem. But what we have seen is that there is a gap in actionable items that any leader can apply consistently to enhance the resilience of their team.

Once armed with a strong motivation, a leader is generally ready to take on the task of becoming more resilient. Through years of research and interaction with leaders at all levels, we have identified six habits that are actionable and impactful.

1. TRUST

Build relationships based on mutual trust. If your team does not trust you, you cannot succeed.

2. INQUISITIVENESS

Every perspective has value. Be present, ask questions, and listen deliberately.

3. HUMILITY

Galvanize the collaboration of those around you to achieve great results. Humility is not modesty but the understanding that one person alone cannot do the job.

4. OPTIMISM

Believe that hard work will lead to positive outcomes.

5. COURAGE

Have the courage to push into zones of discomfort, necessary for individual, team, and organizational growth. It takes courage to follow your convictions. Defining moments will arise when your values conflict with those of others.

6. DISCIPLINE

Establish what needs to be done, decree consequences, and take action in a disciplined manner. Great leaders master personal discipline in key aspects of their lives.

Habitual Practices and Setback Strategies

If resilient leadership were easy, we would see much more evidence of it. Countless leaders have ambitiously set out to change the way they lead. Yet few make changes that are enduring. Building new habits is a difficult thing. It requires repetition until new pathways are created in our brain. And while we are building these new pathways, it is common to face setbacks. It takes great tenacity to redefine, on a permanent basis, how we lead—and requires having the discipline to stick with it and the ability to reengage when we face setbacks.

THE NEED AND MOTIVATION TO CHANGE

Looking in the mirror and accepting the need to change is easier said than done. Only by embracing the need to lead differently—and identifying a strong, personal motivation to be a better leader—will you be able to make the change.

Some years ago, the board of directors of a labor relations organization asked us to work with one of their senior vice presidents, "Anthony." Anthony was one of the foremost labor relations experts in Canada, recognized across the country for his knowledge and skill. So, when the CEO position became vacant, he was the natural candidate. He knew the industry and the players, and was a master of his craft. To the surprise of many, the board rejected him as a candidate, instead appointing the CFO, who hadn't even applied.

You can imagine how this sat with our new client. He felt hurt, verging on insulted. He felt betrayed by his employer and questioned what more he could have done to earn the top job.

And this was our entry point: working with an individual who felt wronged and who struggled to hear what the board was saying—that he lacked the soft skills to lead the team and the industry.

Anthony was one of the most intelligent people I had ever met. When we walked him through the six habits of resilient leaders and asked him to consider himself against them, he was quickly able to see where the gaps existed. He had the first part right: willingness to change.

But, as we got into the attributes and behavioral changes that were required, he became fixated on demonstrating to the board that he was growing and learning, and that he would soon be ready to take on the position. He knew what he wanted:

to be the CEO of the organization. We struggled with this. It was a motivation that felt hollow. We were concerned that he would get the top job and revert to his old behaviors. His motivation was wrong.

"Anthony," I said, "I'm not sure we can help you. If your sole motivation is to get the CEO job, I think we should stop. What happens if you don't get it? Or worse, what happens if you do? If this is all an exercise to prove to someone that you've learned a new trick, it won't be sustainable. You need to think about your motivation. Because if it is all about a promotion, we are the wrong people to help you."

The meeting did not end well. Faces were red, heart rates were elevated, and some unpleasantries were exchanged. So we decided to let it sit for a few days, then Anthony would let us know how he wanted to proceed.

Five days of radio silence ensued. I assumed that we had lost the client. And then the phone rang. It was Anthony. His voice was shaking. "Can you talk?" he asked.

When we met the next day, we witnessed a vulnerability unlike anything we had experienced before or since. Anthony shared that he had done five days of soul searching. In that time, he concluded that he had attached his identity to his position and that this needed to change. He went on to express that he felt he had some significant gifts but that he was standing in his own way. He shared his belief that, if harnessed, these gifts could enable the transformation of an industry. He acknowledged that he wanted to be the next CEO. But whether he got that job or not, it was more important to him to be able to say that he was setting an example for his daughter as someone who relentlessly pursued being the best version of himself, and that he was creating an environment for those around him to excel.

Wow! This was for real.

Anthony embraced the learning like no one we had seen before. His motivation was grounded in purpose, and this made all the difference. He has gone on to be the best CEO the organization has ever had. When he took on the role of CEO, the organization's measure of employee engagement stood at 24 percent. Less than three years later, it had improved to over 75 percent.

Anthony provided us with great learning. Knowing what good leadership is and wanting it for the right reasons are two very different things. It is the willingness and positive motivation for change that makes the opportunity for learning and growth a reality.

Willingness and motivation are the starting points. From there, leaders need to understand and apply the attributes of resilient leadership.

The Habits of Resilient Leaders in Action

If the six habits of resilient leaders outlined earlier in this chapter sound simple to you, I want to assure you that enacting them daily in your life is anything but. The first thing a leader needs to do before taking action is to look in the mirror, so to speak, and do a rigorous self-assessment. If that leader decides to take up the challenge, they won't be able to do it in a vacuum. A leader embarking on this journey will need to interact with experts to best understand the habits and learn how to refine the ways in which they will be applied. They will then test them out in trial-and-error situations. Do you recall the hours I spent with a box of doughnuts in the lunchroom, learning to connect with my coworkers? That was a real-life test-drive of the second habit—inquisitiveness—which quickly helped show me the shape of the others, like trust and humility. With perseverance and a bit of good fortune, a leader who continues to study the habits and who is rigorous with their trial-and-error will eventually be ready to apply them daily. It takes time, dedication, courage, tenacity, and fortitude. It is hard work. And it is this rigorous boot-camp process, combined with the power of the applied habits, that enables resilient leadership. These habits have been tested with dozens of leaders. We have watched those leaders struggle and, more often than not, we have watched them enjoy the incredible experience of leading a team of highly engaged people who aspire to be the best versions of themselves. And we've seen that those who apply them consistently get the best results.

We all exist somewhere on the continuum for each of the individual habits (Trust, Inquisitiveness, Humility, Optimism, Courage, Discipline). You might be a master of humility. You might be a great listener. But very few people are masters of them all. As mentioned, leaders who work on growing the habits versus aspiring to the next position get far better results. But embracing these habits with the motivation is hard work. It requires discipline (one of the habits) and, as with all changes worth making, the fortitude to stick with it. And, despite best intentions, everyone wobbles. So, before you begin your journey, make a plan, and, equally important, a plan to get back on track when you falter.

Below I'm going to share two case studies that illustrate the different and impactful ways the habits can be applied in a time of crisis. These are real-life examples from real people doing the best they could in difficult circumstances. In 2020 during the COVID-19 pandemic, we had the opportunity to work with

It is important to acknowledge that significant psychological factors are at play for all of us, and that some people, whether it be because of nature or nurture, will not be capable of embracing all of these habits. Personality disorders like narcissism and psychopathy, for example, tend to make individuals incapable of resilient leadership because of the clinical aspects that come with those conditions. Superiority complex, arrogance, remorselessness, and lack of empathy are common among people who suffer from disorders like these. For others, psychological challenges like low stress tolerance, impulse control, or insecurity may stand in the way of their withstanding the rigors of resilient leadership. For these people, only clinical counseling and, in extreme cases, institutional support, will allow them the psychological mindset to embrace resilient leadership. We have encountered these situations on our journey. If you are struggling to embrace the habits of resilient leaders, you might consider working with a counselor or a psychologist. They can help.

two family-owned enterprises in the business-to-consumer segment. One was regional, based in Western Canada, and the other was national, based in Central Canada. Both had significant overhead burdens linked to real estate and sales staff. Both were facing the same reality that their traditional distribution was going to be impacted dramatically, if not catastrophically. Ignite provided CEO advisory and strategy services to both organizations. Yet the CEOs heard and reacted to the feedback in very different ways.

CASE STUDY

THE REGIONAL COMPANY

The newly minted CEO of this company, "Terry," had made it his intention to be the best leader he could be. He accepted that his job was to build on the legacy of his father and grandfather as he led the company through its next phase, one which would be defined by "leadership through people" and the creation of a highly motivated team. Terry had participated in creating a statement of purpose for the family, their legacy. He saw himself as the steward of that legacy, and he was highly motivated to honor the generations before him and those that would follow.

Terry recognized that he had a lot to learn. He engaged a coach, he communicated regularly with his family, and, most importantly, he listened to his people.

When the COVID-19 pandemic hit, Terry was staring down the barrel of a gun, so to speak. The early numbers were clear. He was positioned to be the CEO who oversaw the demise of the family business. But rather than panic in crisis, he assembled his team, gathered as much information as possible, and very deliberately went forward to make changes predicated on:

1. Health and well-being of staff
2. Care and concern for customers
3. Long-term viability of the business

Layoffs were inevitable. But rather than make across-the-board cuts, Terry and his team considered areas where they had been inefficient in the past and dug deeper there. They also recognized that the industry would be shifting to some form of online delivery. Terry invested there. And, most importantly, he acted with care and compassion.

Six months into the crisis, he was able to report that the company had returned to profitability. Then, as the nine-month mark hit, he opined that the crisis had presented him and the organization with what they needed to become a national dominant force. This company is well on its way to being aligned with the 9 percent referred to in the 2010 *Harvard Business Review* article that had better results postrecession than prerecession.

CASE STUDY

THE NATIONAL COMPANY

This situation was vastly different from the one just described above. The owner, "Joanne," who had been outside the business for the preceding ten years, had been drawn back in. It was not where she wanted to be. Her CEO had left earlier in the year and a short tenure with a new president had not worked out. She was what we would refer to as a "reluctant leader." Twenty-first-century leadership was not her calling. She had shepherded the company through an era of prosperity in the 1990s before handing off the reins. In the ensuing years, she had focused on philanthropy and governance of the organization. Joanne is a wonderful woman. She cares about people.

But she did not want to be where she found herself, and her leadership reflected that.

In the months before the COVID-19 pandemic, Joanne's efforts were centered on relearning the business. She had a tendency to be somewhat distrustful, and she questioned everything and everyone. The executive team felt that they were not being heard. Departures started to occur. The culture of the organization was gradually shifting to one of fear, the great hindrance of resiliency.

By the time the pandemic was eight months in, more than half of the executive team had left. Losses were mounting, and those who remained were seeking exit plans.

The story, fortunately, has a happy ending. Joanne started to shift her thinking. She realized that her approach wasn't working. She shared that she had endured many sleepless nights and that she knew it was she who needed to change. Finally, in what was likely the hardest thing she ever had to do as an executive, she ceded control to her team. While this national company is unlikely to align with the 9 percent referenced earlier, it is still on the path to regain much of its lost ground. And that is, to a great extent, because Joanne embraced two critical habits of resilient leaders: trust and humility.

The above case studies highlight how two leaders in very similar circumstances led differently and achieved vastly different results. They also provide an excellent canvas to showcase the habits of resilient leaders. Suffice it to say, Terry had proved to be a master of resilient leadership. Joanne, conversely, recognized that leadership, at this time in her life, was not her calling and, with humility and trust in her people, transitioned control. Oddly enough, this proved in its own way to also be an enduring example of resilient leadership. There is more than one way to be a resilient leader.

I'm sure that as you read this book you're identifying the areas in which you have good leadership instincts. You might even work with a team that does well because of you. But are you a great leader? Do you want to be? We hope you take the time do a rigorous self-assessment and give yourself the opportunity to apply some of the constructs in this book to enhance your leadership. Your team needs you.

RESILIENCE IN THE FACE OF CRISIS

Through COVID-19, my team and I at Ignite Management Services came to understand that while resilience may not feel particularly important when times are good, it is essential when times are bad.

In January 2020, we were tremendously optimistic. We had finished 2019 strong and were looking forward to a record-setting year. This optimism led us to act on our plan for growth. We hired more people and rented a new space five times the size of our former office to serve our growing client base. On March 9, 2020, we moved into the new space with great anticipation. Then, on March 13, 2020, COVID-19 was declared a global pandemic, and on that same day we sent our staff home; our new space was nothing more than a hope for better days. In the ensuing eight weeks, things went from good to bad to worse. It started with clients who had committed to engaging us later in the year pulling back. The growth we were anticipating was gone. And then the realities of the pandemic hit our current clients and our monthly revenue fell by 40 percent. We were staring down catastrophic monthly losses.

I know that many others faced a similar reality through COVID-19. Many had it far worse than we did. Nonetheless, the viability of keeping our team together was in doubt. Suddenly, optimism sounded almost delusional, and we were forced to step back and question what we really mean by optimism and resilience. Our business recognizes optimism as a core habit of resilient leadership. It was now being put to the test in real time. We first learned what optimism is not.

- It is not ignoring the realities of the moment and believing they will go away.
- It is not about a demonstration of positivity.
- It is not blind faith.

Optimism is about hard work. It is about confronting the realities—no matter how daunting—and dealing with them, head-on. It is about believing that this work will pay off in the end.

As we are emerging from the COVID-19 era, it is time to reflect. And I do this with a profound sense of pride in my team.

For context, Ignite is a small business. It is the primary source of income for my family, and it is our retirement plan. Losing it would have been devastating. And, admittedly, I wavered. There were days when I wasn't my best. There were days when I was certainly my worst. And there were days when I felt very alone and wanted to give up. During those days, I learned something else about resilience. It is not something you can have alone. It was on these dark days that my teammates gave me purpose and resolve. This became the next key learning: Resilience is a team endeavor. We cannot do it alone.

My colleagues, also, had every opportunity to cocoon, to give up. But they chose a different path. We were clear and honest with our staff and shared our reality throughout the pandemic, including information about financial losses and how long we could sustain them. The team rallied. We recognized early on that we needed to shift how we operated. We isolated the areas we needed to change and improve and set goals for our team to achieve. Each team member committed to their role and to these new goals. The pandemic year became the most successful year we have ever had.

Through this exercise, we learned that resilience is about embracing difficult situations as learning opportunities—moments to take stock, create a plan, and enact it, becoming better and stronger along the way. This is essentially our Inform, Align, Act paradigm that we've been offering clients for more than a decade. (See chapter 4, page 48.) To see the paradigm in action in such a time of crisis was profound.

Finally, what was truly reinforced throughout the pandemic is that optimism is a driving force of resiliency. It was our team's optimism that carried us through those dark days.

TWO

MOTIVATION

ALI

*At the center of your being you have the answer;
you know who you are and you know what you want.*

LAO-TZU

A S A KID, I wanted to be a spy. I don't know where the motivation came from. However, it went away almost as quickly as it came, replaced by desire to be a writer, then a doctor, then a surgeon, and then a lawyer... It wasn't until the summer after my first year at university that the idea of being a spy reemerged. I was agitated and restless, and I decided to act upon my urge. I made an appointment at an army reserve unit in my hometown, but in the interim, I convinced myself that my being a spy was a silly idea and I canceled the appointment. I carried on with university and mostly didn't think about being a spy (intelligence officer or special forces operator, by then), but the idea would occasionally resurface. In post-university professional life, each time I became restless, I would gravitate back to the idea. But I kept convincing myself it was an unrealistic fantasy; being a spy or super-soldier was not a real job for real people, I thought. Finally, at age thirty-two, sick of my waffling, I applied to be an officer in the navy. Five months later, I was sworn in. Five months after that, I completed basic training. In the end I didn't become a spy, but I did follow through on my motivation. I became a soldier (and sailor) for three years.

This is one story of many in my journey of self-discovery and growth. My motivation, as I later realized, didn't have much to do with being a spy. It was about the call to adventure, listening to the whisperings of the heart, and pushing myself to do scary things. It was about growth. And I've since understood that the process of growth is my source of joy and fulfillment. As psychologist Mihaly Csikszentmihalyi says in his book *Flow: The Psychology of Optimal Experience*, "The best moments [in life] occur when a person's body or mind is stretched to its limits in a voluntary effort to accomplish something difficult and worthwhile."[1]

It is through growth that I have found a motivating purpose, and I believe that through this growth I've inspired those around me to understand and develop themselves and find their own purpose, leading them to more fulfilling and joyful lives.

Daniel Pink, author of *Drive: The Surprising Truth about What Motivates Us*, argues that purpose is critical to motivation.[2] Motivation is situational and drives us toward a particular goal—money, praise, status, fulfillment, and personal gratification, to name a few. While these motivators play a role in moving us forward, purpose is about something bigger and more important than ourselves. It is universal and drives us across different areas of our lives. Purpose is what enables a person to stay the course in times of difficulty or crisis; purpose is what kicks in when situational motivation is not enough. As an example, in my first week of basic training, three members of my platoon left voluntarily. I suspect their motivations for being there were not tied to purpose—perhaps they were there for the pension or to satisfy their parents—and so did not have a compelling reason to persevere. As leaders, we must be driven by a sense of purpose, because the role is inherently one of challenge and discomfort. Without purpose, a leader will surely falter in those instances that require resilience.

This book can tell you what it means to be a resilient leader and why it matters for organizations, but it can't tell you why it matters to *you*. When you look within, what do you see? Only you can look inward, know who you are, and know what you want. You read earlier about how Anthony found purpose and how this was instrumental in enabling him to grow; how he looked within, studied his approach, learned, and changed. It is only through a deeply personal motivation for pursuing leadership, tied to purpose, that a person will have a genuine willingness to change and the ability to authentically embody the traits of resilient leadership.

Finding a Motivating Purpose

The good news is that there is no single purpose that you are meant to discover. In fact, you will more than likely have different purposes at different stages of your life. But what truly matters is that you discover a motivating purpose. How important is it? Important enough that it has been proven that those who wake up in the morning with a clear idea of what they are doing and why they are doing it are healthier, happier, and live longer than those who don't.[3] And you can find purpose in what you're doing today. For instance, helping others realize their potential could be your purpose for leadership. So too can setting an example for your kids or contributing to your community.

John Herdman, Ignite client and head coach of the Canadian men's soccer team, suggests asking yourself three questions to connect with your motivating purpose: *What do I want? Why do I want it? Who do I want it for?*

What do I want? is generally the easiest of the three to answer, but I'd offer, as a companion to this query, another question: *What do I want most?*

We can't have it all, at least not all at the same time. In the first decade of my career, I struggled to accept the opportunity cost of my choices. I wanted to take all paths. I still do, though to a lesser degree. And so it is important to not only ask what you want but also to prioritize what you want when your desires conflict.

The question *Why do I want it?* can be frustratingly difficult to answer. As a mentor told me recently, "Our minds are adept at hiding our true motivations." The constant pressure from outside forces (society, parents, peers, social media) makes it difficult to listen to and know ourselves. There isn't one right reason to pursue leadership, but you must be honest with yourself about your motivation. A leader might say they want the promotion to better provide for their family, but they may already have more than enough. Another might say they want to be the CEO of the family business because it's what's best for the organization, but their sister would do just as well. Both are examples where we have encouraged people to dig deeper to explore and understand their true motivation.

In answering *Why do I want it?* consider the Five Whys technique, invented by Sakichi Toyoda, founder of Toyota Industries, and designed to find the root cause of a problem. The point of the technique is that you continue asking why until you get to the truth of your motivation. Only *you* can pull

back the layers of expectations and preconceptions to reach
that truth. And only with a true motivating purpose will you
show up authentically.

The question *Who do I want it for?* helps you confront
the truth behind your motivation. Is it to make your parents
happy? Is it to prove people wrong? The question also helps
focus you on service to others. If purpose is to give meaning
to our lives, it must be bigger than ourselves. As Grand Slam
champion Arthur Ashe said, "From what we get, we can make
a living; what we give, however, makes a life."[4]

Willingness to Change

There isn't a single person who is born a resilient leader. And
to become one requires that you embrace change, which first
means that you must become aware that you need to change.
Then, you must find a motivating purpose that creates a genuine willingness to change. And finally, you must understand
how to change.

For years I struggled with muscle imbalances in my shoulders and back. Several massage therapists and physiotherapists
identified the problem and prescribed a handful of stretching
and strengthening exercises. I'd do them for a while, then quit.
The problem kept getting worse. One day I saw a new therapist.
She didn't conclude anything different from what others had
but delivered the message in a way that hit me hard: "If you
don't do something about this right now," she said, "you're
going to have a serious problem." There was no lightness to
her tone that I could use to let myself off the hook. She didn't
give me a few easy exercises to do, as the others did, expecting
that this would correct a years-old problem. She referred me
to a personal trainer and told me to invest in it. I cried, then I

called the trainer and began working diligently to correct my weaknesses. I finally understood that I must change, I decided I wanted to, and I got help.

A few years ago, I worked with the leader of a midsized apparel company who was trying, desperately, to dig her company out of a toxic work environment. Over the preceding years, beginning before her time at the company, a culture of bullying, gossip, and infighting had developed. The leader was in a tailspin and spent most of our early conversations talking about the other executives and their bad behavior. She stated her willingness to change. She acknowledged that she might be part of the problem and was maybe even the wrong leader for the business. Yet it was impossible to engage her in a meaningful conversation about her leadership. She was completely focused on the behavior of others.

I remember her calling me halfway through our engagement. She sounded at peace and in charge. Something had shifted. "I've just realized that I'm the problem," she said, "and I have to be the solution." She was excited by this revelation. It was like the clouds had parted and she suddenly saw the light. But, of course, she didn't suddenly arrive at this new perspective. She came to it through a deep process of seeking to understand the experiences of others in the organization, engaging an external adviser, and refusing to give up in the quest for a solution. She had entered the engagement with a willingness to change, but it was only when she focused on what was in her control—her own behavior and actions—that she was able to change the organization. And she did. Months later, she reported that it felt like a different company.

In both leadership and in life, change starts with *you*, and, in a leadership context, your behavior is the single biggest determinant of the culture of your company. Structure, systems, and processes have an impact, but nothing has a greater impact than the leaders. Show us a culture with a lack of accountability and we'll show you senior leaders not holding people accountable. Show us a culture of learning and we'll show you senior leaders who celebrate making mistakes. It isn't easy to accept that you are both problem and solution. And harder still to find the courage to change. But as the famous stoic philosopher Seneca said, "If you really want to escape the things that harass you, what you're needing is not to be in a different place but to be a different person."[5]

Change is a choice. It may be catalyzed by an outside force—a superior (or therapist) telling you that you must change, losing a job, or finding yourself at the bottom of a pit that only you can pull yourself out of—or by an internal force: realizing that you are not the person or leader you want to be, and deciding to do something about it.

Some will choose to change before it becomes necessary. Others still will never change and will suffer the disappointment of a life unrealized.

The Leadership Choice

The choice to grow as a leader is yours, and yours alone. Leadership is not a burden but a challenge, and like any challenge, it will test you and ultimately present an opportunity to give your life meaning.

With a personal and motivating purpose, and a willingness and a desire to change, any of us can build the habits of resilient leaders. But each individual must still make a conscious choice to pursue leadership. You must decide whether leadership is what you want.

In our work, we see a range of perspectives on the role of a leader, but it can generally be broken down into two extremes. At one end, there is a group that sees their role as helping people reach their potential and helping the organization achieve results through people. They see their first job as leading and motivating others, and that is their focus. At the other end, there is a group that never truly embraces the role of people leader. They see their first job as driving business results and have not embraced the idea that leadership of people is the path to achieving those results.

MOTIVATED TO CHANGE

In our early work with Terry, who you'll recall from our case study in chapter 1, we spent a great deal of time exploring his motivation to embrace resilient leadership. This exploration followed what had been, for him, a very difficult period. The organization had never had a CEO. Instead, Terry and his sibling had run the business on a consensus basis. This worked in the short term. But fissures were developing. The pair was experiencing differences of opinion and, gradually, the sense of Team One was diminishing. The family engaged in an exercise to craft a clear statement of purpose, a "legacy statement." And they recognized that for the company to be in service to that legacy, it needed a CEO. It could be Terry or his sibling. But it couldn't be both.

Ultimately, the family chose Terry to be the CEO. And, fortunately, he understood the magnitude of the challenge that lay in front of him. There had been acrimony. There were differing loyalties. There was enterprise confusion. And he was a first-time CEO.

Terry had a gift many leaders don't have. He was willing to confront his shortcomings. He had already accepted the need to change, learn, and grow. The next step was to underpin this desire to change with a powerful motivation that would allow him to stick with it.

After much soul searching, Terry became clear on his purpose. His grandfather and father had created a company that cared about the well-being of people and community. The family had stated clearly in their legacy that they wanted this to continue. Terry's motivation was to grow his leadership to enable him to effectively steward the family legacy for generations.

CASE STUDY

NOT MOTIVATED TO CHANGE

Joanne, who you'll also recognize from chapter 1, was not a first-time CEO. She had led her organization for nearly a decade. But she had handed over the reins to a new CEO and entered semi-retirement. When the CEO left, efforts to replace her were problematic and Joanne was drawn back into the business. It was not the same company she had handed off. She took over at a time when there was considerable divisiveness at the executive table. Arguably, there was a talent gap. The team was not functioning at a high level, and this was impacting operations.

Joanne had a leadership style that was based on her experience a decade earlier. What she led then was a much smaller, less complex entity. The world of digital distribution had become a driving force and it was new to her. In her prior time as CEO, she would make decisions based on an instinctive knowledge of how the industry worked. And she was successful. But now, she needed the expertise of her team and was frustrated when it didn't appear to be there.

Joanne realized that she was not motivated to lead the changes that were required in this organization, and she did the right thing. She ceded control to her executive and replaced herself as president.

LEADERSHIP IS NOT a given. Whether a person was promoted into a leadership role or founded a business and now oversees hundreds or thousands of people, that does not make them a leader. Leadership—the leadership of people to help them reach their potential—is a choice. And it is a choice you must decide whether you want or not. Before continuing to chapter 3, we encourage you to pause, look within, and ask (and answer) these questions:

What do I want?

What do I want most?

Why do I want it?

Who do I want it for?

THREE

TRUST

MIKE

Nobody cares how much you know,
until they know how much you care.

THEODORE ROOSEVELT

TRUST IS a central part of all human relationships. Living creatures constantly scan the environment for cues of safety or threat. The neuromechanisms that guide this involuntary process run in the background constantly as an evolutionary and biological fact. Trust is the belief that someone is good, honest, safe, and reliable. Critically, it is the belief that they will not cause you harm. Trust is therefore bidirectional: it is something to be given and something to be earned on an individual basis. Status or positional authority do not create trust. Only interpersonal experiences will enable trust, and the deeper those experiences, the stronger the trust bond will be. Finally, trust is both a catalyst and an enabler of resiliency; it enhances our ability to respond to changes that are taking place around us.

Given the rate of change in today's business landscape, people are being continually thrust into positions of discomfort as they face the reality of what change looks like. It may be that a person is competent at their job but, because of change, they *feel* less competent. Situations like this cause uncertainty and doubt. People in this position will naturally look to their leader for confidence that they can succeed. Employees' ability to believe in themselves is significantly enhanced when they trust their leader.

Trustworthy leaders bring significant benefits to their organization and their colleagues, including greater employee engagement, retention, and performance. And when trust is low, employees are less committed, less engaged, and less likely to take initiative or innovate. In 2002, researchers from Washington University in St. Louis and State University of New York at Buffalo analyzed research from 106 studies and found that higher job satisfaction and higher commitment were both linked to trust in leaders.[1]

Also in 2002, a research team at Cornell University surveyed more than 6,500 employees at 76 U.S. and Canadian Holiday Inn hotels to identify the level of trust employees had in their managers. The survey responses were then correlated to customer satisfaction surveys, personnel records, and financial records. The link between high trust and high profitability was so strong that a one-eighth-point improvement in the trust score could be expected to increase profitability by a whopping 2.5 percent.[2]

According to *Harvard Business Review*, research conducted for *Fortune*'s "100 Best Companies to Work For" found that "trust between managers and employees is the primary defining characteristic of the very best workplaces" and that these companies "beat the average annualized returns of the s&p 500 by a factor of three."[3]

With trust being fundamental to personal and organizational health and success, it is critical to establish trust bonds

Reflect for a moment on a time in your life when trust was lost or taken away, or when the bond of trust was broken. Now, compare that with how you feel when you are part of a deep trust bond. It isn't hard to see why trust is one of the single most impactful and important things a leader needs to develop with the individuals they are leading.

with colleagues. A breach in trust, especially at the leadership level, can have those you lead lose their motivation, spontaneity, reciprocity, curiosity, openness, exploration, and creativity. And once that trust is broken, the relationship ruptures.

I will always remember a profound moment in my career when I broke a bond of trust with someone who worked for me. I was relatively new in a role, and he was the leader of an important division. I needed him to succeed for the organization to succeed. And, in my haste to gain his support, I promised a promotion if we were successful.

As time wore on, it became apparent that he was already in the right position and that a promotion would not serve him or the organization well. I sat down with him the evening before he left for vacation and told him that there would be no promotion and that he should use the upcoming two weeks to reevaluate his career. It was a cringeworthy performance that haunts me to this day. Both what I said and how I said it were devastating to him. The trust bond was broken forever. We still know one another. And while I hope his pain has softened, one thing is for certain: he will never put full faith in me again. I also suspect he became much less trusting with those who followed me in that role.

Trust is easy to talk about. Its importance is equally easy to demonstrate. But building deep trust is hard work. It needs to be deliberate. It requires introspection, and it requires action.

The Five Cs of Trust

Care, Communication, Character, Consistency, and Competence. These are the five Cs to live by when it comes to establishing and building trust.

Care

While a leader must be above average on each of the five Cs to be effective, growing evidence suggests that care matters more than the others.

Many leaders engage in unconscious acts of self-destruction in their first days in a new job. They do this by making change too quickly, by telling versus asking, and by not engaging the hearts and minds of the people around them. All of this can lead one to be seen as uncaring, and if you are seen as such, you will not build trust. If you don't build trust, you will not engage hearts and minds. If you don't engage hearts and minds, your results will be suboptimal.

Here is some practical advice for leaders:

1. Embrace care as a personal value. Accept that it is the foundation of trust. Model it and recruit people who demonstrate it.

2. Establish a personal accountability to get to know the people who report to you.

3. Learn what is important to the people who report to you.

4. Work with them to draw links between what is important to them and their careers.

The best example I have seen in demonstrating care in the workplace comes from a former board colleague, Shauneen Bruder. Shauneen, recently retired from the position of executive vice president and head of Operations at Royal Bank of Canada, provided oversight to systems and processes for one of the world's preeminent financial institutions.

When I joined the board of directors of the Canadian Chamber of Commerce on a one-year appointment, Shauneen was chair of the board. The day after I accepted the position, I received an unexpected phone call from her. Receiving that call—a call from one of the most powerful women in the country—left me stunned. I'll never forget her words. "I am delighted to have you join the board. You will bring a perspective we really need."

Wow. Did she need to make the call? No. Was I important to the chamber? Marginally. So why did she call? I learned, through years of working with Shauneen, that she called because she cared. She cared about the perspectives of others. She cared about how they felt. And she knew that cohesion was a critical part of a high-performance team. In every interaction, Shauneen would build trust.

What, you might ask, was the point of her investing this time? She said it best: "We should talk about followership, not leadership. We must earn the right for people to follow us. It doesn't come from position or personality. It comes from your deliberate effort to earn the right to have them follow you. And it is their gift to you when they bring their energy in pursuit of your vision."[4]

Communication

It is one thing to care. It is quite another to communicate with care. The importance of this was really driven home through an engagement we had with a midsized manufacturing organization. The CEO was one of the brightest leaders we have had an opportunity to work with. He had overseen a significant turnaround. By all indications, he was a trusted leader.

And then things changed. The manager of the hedge fund that owned the organization told the CEO it was time to prepare the business for sale. They wanted to see costs contained and to transition to a near-singular focus on profitability. The CEO accepted this new direction. Regrettably, though, the shift in mandate carried with it a shift in leadership style. A new sense of urgency had crept into his approach. A command-and-control period ensued. Meeting after meeting, email after email, the focus of communication was financial results. Initiatives were created to drive short-term revenue. People were directed to reduce expenses. Often these initiatives were diametrically opposed. The program wasn't working, and it was time for an intervention.

The CEO invited Ignite in to help him assess what was happening. We affirmed his concerns. Silos had developed. Skepticism had crept in. Confidence was falling and, perhaps most importantly, for the first time, the team was not trusting him. The intervention demonstrated, with an abundance of clarity, the critical role communication plays in building trust. The CEO had taken direction from the board and had immediately assimilated it into his accountability framework. This, in turn, cascaded through the organization. But there was a missing ingredient. His team did not know why things were changing and had not been engaged and given an opportunity to process the path they were to follow. He assumed that they would immediately follow the new path. Why wouldn't they? They had always been with him before. He had *told* them about the new direction and assumed they would follow.

Telling is not communicating. Communication requires active listening and understanding. It requires engaging at the level of personal pursuits.

Fortunately, this story has a happy ending. In the planning retreat that formed part of the intervention, the CEO led off with three of the most important words he had ever uttered. "Shame on me," he said to his team. "Shame on me for not asking for your advice as we went down this path. Shame on me."[5] And, with that show of vulnerability and honesty, he started a dialogue that saw the full team recommit in full alignment with board expectations.

The business was ultimately sold. And when it was, I got to watch as the CEO said goodbye to his colleagues (the business was rolled under the purview of the new parent company and his role had become redundant). There was not a dry eye in the room.

That there were tears was interesting. They were reflective of an incredible journey that had good times and bad. And they reflected the truths that had been shared along the way. The CEO had always communicated honestly. But he had not always communicated with care. When that changed, so too did trust. Great leaders do not shy away from providing honest feedback, both positive and negative. They are as comfortable providing this feedback to their superiors as they are with subordinates because they view all people on this planet as equals. The critical component of successful feedback is that you are sharing openly your beliefs with a view to helping others succeed.

Through years of watching how leaders communicate and the results that follow, we have identified a small number of best practices:

1. Tell the truth.

2. Be direct. Better to say the right thing the wrong way than to say nothing at all.

3. Always start a difficult conversation with the mindset that you care about the individual you are speaking with.

4. Link your communication to your organizational vision wherever possible. Never let your team lose sight of the defining purpose of your organization.

Character

In 2019, I had the pleasure of attending the convocation for the Harvard Business School MBA class. Dean Nitin Nohria shared these thoughts with graduates:

> It is tempting to think you can get away with the half-truth. The occasional straying over the line, the zigs and zags away from your own espoused values or those of your organization. But these lapses inevitably accumulate and catch up with you. Even if they are not discovered by others, they will make your achievements seem hollow. When character lapses are discovered by others, the consequences are devastating.

They destroy careers, damage firms, and add a significant dent in society's trust in business and its leaders.[6]

Dean Nohria's comments rang true to me. Think about the punishment society doles out through social media for public figures whose character or integrity is called into question. The things we do today will be on record decades from now. Like it or not, we must accept it. This is our reality.

But more important than how people we don't know view us is how we are seen by those who do know us—our families, our friends, and our colleagues. They see what we do. And their trust in us will be a function of the integrity that we display.

A common challenge we see is the leader who has more than one persona. These leaders often display a "work face" at the office and a "friend or family face" with others. At its core, this demonstrates a lack of authenticity, and in these situations we encourage our clients to go back and reflect on their motivation and purpose. The reason they cannot be their authentic self in all interactions likely rests here. If their motivation or purpose is hollow and they are unwilling to do the deep searching within that is required of a resilient leader, it will be almost impossible for that leader to create deep trust.

Character best enables trust for those leaders who understand themselves and show up honestly as their true self. A terrific example of this is a CEO we worked with who led an organization that employed over seven thousand people. He was appointed to the role in the twilight of his career. He was an unassuming man—not gregarious and not someone who could be referred to as charismatic. But he was true to himself. He was brought in as a bridge CEO. So here was this quiet, unassuming man taking over the reins of an organization that had been through incredible turbulence, and with much more on the horizon. Most expected a placeholder and hoped, at best, that the organization would be stable during his tenure. What happened provided me with a gift of learning that I will be forever grateful for. He accepted the role, and, after about ninety days, he laid it out for his executive team.

"I've been thirty-seven years with this organization," he said. "I started as a junior accountant, and I never dreamed I would be sitting in this chair. I will be retiring in two years. I have grandchildren coming, and I want to enjoy a healthy retirement with my family. But I want to be able to look back and say that the organization was left better than it was when I took on the role."

He had no delusions of grandeur. Gave no great speech. He simply and humbly shared his hopes. He went on to say, "When I'm gone, I want the board to see us as a highly functioning team, and I want each of you to grow in your roles to ensure that one of you becomes my natural replacement. I want to ensure that we have clarity of vision that will drive our activities long after I am gone."[7]

He was not the first leader to share a plan. However, his presentation was different. He shared it from a very personal place. This was to be his legacy, and he allowed others to truly feel what he was feeling. When he retired, it was with the inner peace that comes when you have been authentic from your first day on the job to the day you leave.

We have one tip for leaders when it comes to character: Behave in a way that would withstand the scrutiny of a front-page newspaper article written about you. Hold yourself to that standard. People will forgive lapses of competence. But lapses of character are much more difficult to recover from.

Consistency

The temperament of a leader permeates their organization and influences cultural norms. We likely have all seen examples of leaders who have reacted negatively (emotionally or behaviorally) to stress. The very best leaders can channel stress into positive responses such as increased mental focus, healthy urgency, and decisiveness. But when a leader exhibits negative stress responses, it imperils enterprise resilience. A leader with a widely vacillating temperament sends a signal to the organization that such a temperament is acceptable if not even endorsed. And as the behavior takes hold, it becomes part of the culture.

I was guilty of displaying emotional inconsistency in my early career, and it is something I wrestle with to this day. It took me years to recognize that how I show up impacts the teams I work with. An industrial psychologist referred to my emotionality as a creative temperament. A psychiatrist later diagnosed it as clinical depression. Either way, it was part of my personality, which then became an unfortunate part of my leadership. It was described to me once by a courageous employee. "Mike," she said, "when you are on your game, your energy and passion carries the team. But when you are down, we are all walking on eggshells."

I've never forgotten that feedback. My lack of emotional consistency was creating ripple effects throughout the office. People didn't know which version of me was showing up on any given day. This eroded confidence, creativity, and passion.

The point of this story is that while displaying emotional consistency sounds easy, it is anything but. Over the years, leaders not doing so has been a significant deterrent to the resilience of many organizations.

A manufacturing leader we worked with, speaking to his colleagues in an organization that had somewhat of a reactive culture, framed it best. "Calm lets us be prepared for what is coming," he said. "Calm lets us respond rationally when things don't go the way we expect."[8] This was from a man who had arrived in Canada as a refugee from Vietnam in the early 1980s. He had seen his share of trauma. He had been in true life-and-death situations. I'll always remember his words. "Calm is good. Consistent calm is better."

Our advice is this: Establish a band in which you will operate. Keep your emotions in check within this band. Establish protections for yourself so that you can recognize how you are showing up. The consequence of getting this wrong can be dire. If you are prone to mood swings, your people might be reluctant to bring you information for fear of which leader will be greeting them in that moment. This stifles the creativity necessary to be adaptable in these disruptive times.

Again, this is easier said than done. Start by keeping it top of mind that operating within a clear emotional band matters. Mindset is a powerful driver of behavior. This simple positioning will go a long way. And don't hesitate to utilize many of the great tools that exist, like meditation, exercise, proper nutrition, and healthy sleep patterns. Once you have decided consistency is important, create a pathway to ensure it is achievable.

Competence

We have discussed many of the soft skills needed for building trust. However, regardless of how caring, communicative, and consistent a leader may be, they will not establish trust if they are not competent. You must build the knowledge to master your craft. You can't fake competence.

Ken Holland, the NHL general manager of the Edmonton Oilers, built his reputation as the GM of the storied Detroit Red Wings. Under his guidance, the Red Wings went on to more consecutive playoff appearances than any team in NHL history. For many years, Ken had the support of one of the most competent coaches in the game at the time, Mike Babcock (who himself is rebuilding his personal brand after a fall from grace because of questions of character). Before Mike's time behind the bench in Detroit, he approached Ken to tell him that he aspired to coach Detroit one day. At that time, Mike was a highly accomplished coach in minor-pro hockey. He had demonstrated his skill at that level and his intrinsic ability to do much more. He had a brilliant career in front of him. But Ken's response, nonetheless, must have been humbling: "Mike, we don't hire interns to coach the Detroit Red Wings."

Ken was not questioning Mike's character or his intrinsic ability. Rather, he was telling Mike that he had some learning to do before he would be ready. Intrinsic ability wasn't enough. He would require experiential learning to build his competence in the role.

Imagine how Mike must have felt, years later, when he was holding the Stanley Cup above his head, knowing all the work he had done to get to that place.

We are all gifted with a certain level of intrinsic ability. Intelligence, by way of example, can be nurtured, but it is primarily driven by DNA. Intelligence is an example of something that is embedded in us. But what many people miss is that it is experiential skill, coupled with intrinsic ability, that develops true competence. The message to leaders is simple: never stop seeking and embracing opportunities to expand experiential skill.

In my early career as a banker, I made a series of mistakes that led to a substantial write-off for my employer. It was a mistake of such magnitude that I was certain I would be fired. I was mentally preparing for that and had written my letter of resignation. My boss, a true gentleman, carried the baggage of my mistake. He knew my mistakes were a negative reflection on him. He had every opportunity to put the blame on me and walk away unscathed.

I was incredibly anxious when he called me to his office. He asked me to walk him through the entire story, highlighting every step along the way where I might have mitigated or prevented the damage. He asked me what I had learned from it. At the end of the meeting, I had recited a series of missteps that were, in my young mind, unforgivable, and I offered him my resignation. He looked at me and said, "Mike, we have just invested tens of thousands of dollars in building your experiential skill. We're not going to waste that investment." Mr. Busch knew that this mistake was an opportunity to build competence that would serve me and the organization well in years to come. He was one of the greatest managers I ever had.

You must be competent if you are to earn the trust of those around you. The message to all aspiring leaders is to take the time necessary to build your skill. Opportunities will come. And, when they do, be ready for them, having built your résumé through experiential learning.

LET'S BRING ALL of this back to enterprise resiliency. A leader seeks to create environments that enable individuals and organizations to adapt to changing conditions. This will naturally draw people out of their comfort zone. They will be moved into places of discomfort where they look to their leaders to give them the confidence to take the appropriate steps forward. For this to take place, there is a natural need to have trust in leadership.

Creating a high-trust environment is not easy. However, the components are clear: Care, Communication, Character, Consistency, and Competence. Applying these on a day-to-day basis requires powerful commitment. Resiliency depends on it.

FOUR

INQUISITIVENESS

ALI

The test of a first-rate intelligence is the
ability to hold two opposed ideas in the mind at the
same time, and still retain the ability to function.

F. SCOTT FITZGERALD

I T IS impossible for leaders to know everything, and this is
doubly true with the complexity of business today and the
rapid rate of change and disruption in the market. Resilient
leaders are curious, and they know how to ask questions that
lead them to consider new ideas. The act of gathering information, asking for opinions and perspectives, and listening
to the answers is what we mean by "inquisitiveness." Leaders
who ask questions and listen intently to the answers come to
better decisions than those who don't, because those decisions
are informed by multiple perspectives. And by engaging their
team in decisions, they increase the team's ownership over the
decision, which is critical for successful implementation. With
better decisions and more engaged teams, organizations better
navigate uncertainty; they are better able to adapt, which positions them to recover more quickly from external pressures
than nonresilient organizations. Inquisitive leaders go slow so
they can then go fast and in the right direction.

Inform, Align, Act

At Ignite we use a paradigm called Inform, Align, Act, to help our clients understand the perspectives of participants (Inform), create alignment around a path forward (Align), and execute against their plans (Act). The Inform phase is at the heart of the process. We don't come to our clients with solutions. We believe they have the answers. Our job is to help draw those out. Inform relies on the art of asking good questions, listening without judgment, exploring the edges, and resisting the urge to jump to conclusions. It requires patience, humility, and inquisitiveness to step into this space of uncertainty and stay there long enough to gather ideas and perspectives, and to know when it's enough, lest you become stuck forever in the process of information gathering.

The problem we most often see with our clients is that the chief executive will often make significant decisions without the input of their team, resulting in decisions or strategies based on a single perspective—their own.

It takes humility to acknowledge that you don't know everything, and that by leveraging the insights and perspectives of your team you will make better decisions. The power of perspective is supported by research. The award-winning workplace researcher Francesca Gino found that when inquisitiveness is employed, people are less likely to succumb to confirmation bias (looking for information that supports one's beliefs rather than for evidence suggesting one is wrong), leading them to generate more alternatives and make fewer decision-making errors.[1] In another, smaller study, Gino found that groups whose curiosity had been heightened performed better because they shared information more openly and listened more carefully.[2]

It is also the power of perspective that supports the business case for diversity and inclusion. It is one thing to seek out and consider the perspectives at the table, quite another to ensure you have the right perspectives at the table in the first place.

The process of engaging our teams and seeking out their insights and considerations demonstrates that we value their input. And if they see their insights reflected, they will be more supportive of the decision, strategy, or plan.

CASE STUDY

ENGAGING FRESH PERSPECTIVES

In 2020, we worked with the CEO of a leading food processing company in Canada that was evaluating a growth opportunity. The opportunity would require a significant amount of capital investment. The organization had grown 10× in the last decade, and this opportunity would have the organization grow 20× if the project were to proceed. However, the board and owner-ship group were concerned about the ability of the executive team to take the company to this next level. They believed in the intrinsic ability of the team but were concerned about their execution capacity and their experiential skill to bring it home.

The CEO could have tried to sell the board on the project. Instead, he took a different approach. He asked for the insights and considerations of the board and shared with them other concepts and alternatives to consider. He approached them with genuine curiosity and an interest in understanding their perspectives. Because he framed the challenge and sought insights—as opposed to going to the board with a stake in the ground—the resulting strategy had the board's input (and was the better for it), and ultimately, board members were more supportive of the project. Seeing their insights embedded in the final strategy increased their confidence in the executive team.

Why Is Inquisitiveness So Difficult?

In a 1996 *Harvard Business Review* article, American organizational theorist Karl Weick argues that ignorance and knowledge support one another in the service of growth in organizational culture:

> In a fluid world, wise people know that they don't fully understand what is happening at a given moment, because what is happening is unique to that time. They avoid extreme confidence and extreme caution, knowing that either can destroy what organizations need most in changing times, namely, curiosity, openness, and the ability to sense complex problems. The overconfident shun curiosity because they think they know what they need to know. The overcautious shun curiosity for fear it will only deepen their uncertainties. Both the cautious and the confident are closed-minded, which means that neither make good judgments.[3]

The overconfident demonstrate a lack of humility, while the overcautious lack courage. Chapters 5 and 7 of this book delve into the habits of humility and courage. But there are more-nuanced reasons inquisitiveness is so difficult.

Many leaders fear that engaging others in decisions will slow them down. In moments of crisis, time is not on the leader's side, and engaging others adds a step or more to the decision-making process. We know, though, that the time taken to engage perspectives is more than compensated for by the power of good decisions embraced by the team.

Others are afraid of asking for perspectives because they know they might hear something they don't like or agree with, and once the lid is off, it is difficult if not impossible to put back on. At the start of an engagement, I'll often ask the client whether it makes sense to include staff beyond the executive team in the process. The question is sometimes met with hesitation, then a self-aware laugh. They are asking themselves, "Do I really want to know what they think?" These leaders understand that if they ask, they will have to do something with the answers. It's an internal battle between knowing you need the perspectives of others and not *really* wanting those perspectives, because they may force a new direction. This inquisitiveness—obtaining the perspectives of others—does not come naturally to many leaders, but the good ones keep at it, constantly reminding themselves that the perspectives of their team are invaluable, and that if they don't actively engage others, they will miss something. These leaders may not always like what others have to say, but they want to hear it.

Then there are those leaders who are fearless and genuinely want to understand and consider perspectives, but they're not hearing them because they aren't asking the right questions. Or they have given their team the false impression that they've already put a stake in the ground, and no one challenges it. I worked with the COO of an association who was tasked by the board to evaluate alternative structures for the organization. The decision to restructure, and the present question of how it was to be done, would have significant repercussions on the identity and mandate of the organization for decades to come. The COO was not convinced that restructuring was the right decision but felt the board's direction was clear. He recognized the significance of the decision to be made and so believed it was critical to draw out the perspectives of the executive team and individual board members to ensure nothing was missed in the evaluation. It took one phone call with the chair of the board (with the COO present) to understand that the chair was not convinced of the need to restructure either, and was less interested in evaluating alternative structures and more interested in answering whether it should be done at all. This reframed the entire process. The COO told me after the call that, despite regular conversations with the chair on this issue, this was the first time he had really heard his perspective. He had been asking the wrong questions because he assumed the chair had already made up his mind.

Another reason for a lack of inquisitiveness is the "curse of the gifted." Some leaders are often three steps ahead of everyone else; they have processed the pros and cons and come to conclusions before others have had an opportunity to fully understand the question. This is not to say that the gifted or intelligent leader is not in need of other perspectives. They need them as much as anyone else. They are simply moving so fast, cognitively, that they haven't stopped to bring others along with them. There is a saying "If you want to go fast, go alone. If you want to go far, go together." The gifted leader, like the leader concerned about efficiency, must decide whether they want to go fast or far.

Practicing Inquisitiveness

The challenges with inquisitiveness may seem complex, but we can all develop inquisitiveness by practicing the associated behaviors, including slowing down in order to ask good questions, and then listening intently, which together cultivate curiosity.

Curiosity, we should clarify, is not inquisitiveness. Curiosity is a desire to understand that which we do not. It is an innate sense of wonder about oneself, other people, the world, or how things work. It should not be assumed, however, that a curious person seeks out answers to their questions. A leader might be curious about a person's motivations or wonder what might happen if they took a different path, but that doesn't mean they have asked the question. Inquisitiveness is curiosity in action. It is the drive to investigate and seek answers to the questions raised by curiosity.

If you've spent time with children, you'd likely agree that we're born inquisitive. But as we age, our natural inquisitiveness is stifled, whether by self-consciousness and the desire to appear competent, or by the belief that we have nothing to learn from others. While some are genetically more disposed to inquisitiveness than others—or more "open to experience"—we can all learn to be more curious and inquisitive.

The leader must shift their mindset from "I must have the answer" to "I must slow down, ask questions, and seek to understand." This is a significant and difficult shift for many leaders, requiring them to unlearn decades of doing things a certain way.

If you want to foster curiosity and develop inquisitiveness, consider asking "Why?," "What if?," "How might we?," and other open-ended questions; use a two-second rule to resist the urge to respond or fill a silence; ask at least one more question after you think you've understood the situation; and play back what you've heard to ensure you understand before solving or deciding.

Coaching and leadership are strongly linked. I like to define coaching as "the ability to not give the answer." It comes down to learning how to ask better questions. The most common mistake I see leaders make is not asking enough questions. They ask maybe one or two and then jump to conclusions and advice giving. We have been programmed as professionals to solve problems and find solutions. But leaders who don't ask enough questions end up making assumptions that have them solving for the wrong issues. Leaders need to slow down and spend more time establishing reality, through inquisitiveness, before problem solving can begin.

These are skills you can build through training programs. But adding new tools to your tool kit won't make the process any more natural. That requires practice. Inquisitiveness feels unnatural for many because they believe they already know the right answer or are used to pretending they do in order to project confidence or competence, and because of an understandable desire to help, provide advice, or come to a decision. Ultimately, to build inquisitiveness, a leader must accept that it matters and that they need the perspective and buy-in of other people, and they must get comfortable with being uncomfortable.

FIVE

HUMILITY

MIKE

Great leaders are not hung up on accomplishments.
Rather, they bring the right people around them
to make themselves irrelevant.

DOUG ARMSTRONG, GENERAL MANAGER, ST. LOUIS BLUES

THE ST. LOUIS BLUES came into the NHL in 1967. Despite some successes prior to 2019, they had never won a Stanley Cup. The 2018–19 season was starting out to be more of the same. At the halfway point in the campaign, they were mired in last place in the league. Most would have been looking to rebuild the team at that point, sacrificing the season in hopes of a brighter future. But General Manager Doug Armstrong didn't give up on his squad. He made a few roster changes and a coaching change and continued to believe in his core group. In the second half of the season, they showed signs of promise. And, by the end of the season, they were on a tear, winning eight of their last ten games. They progressed through the first three rounds of the playoffs and competed against the legendary Boston Bruins for the Stanley Cup. The series went the full seven games, and, for the first time in its fifty-one-year history, St. Louis won the cup.

What matters here is not that they won, but rather how they did it. It was a team that was driven by a humble leader who truly believed it was the success of others that would dictate his own.

In writing this book, we interviewed some incredible leaders. One of them was Doug Armstrong. I interviewed Doug long before his team won the coveted cup. But after our interview, I said to my colleague, "He will win the Stanley Cup one day." This was not because I liked him (I did), but because he demonstrated the habits of a resilient leader more clearly and resolutely than anyone I had ever met, and he was deliberate in how he applied them. He used more colorful words than most corporate executives we meet, but the concepts were abundantly clear.

Doug spoke about humility when we met. But more importantly, he demonstrated it through his actions as a leader. The example he set cascaded through the organization. The Stanley Cup playoffs are a battle of endurance. The victors *always* work well as a team. Each player is *always* clear on his role. And they *always* support one another to the final whistle. You will see this in every team that has ever won this trophy. Doug's humility set the example and encouraged others to internalize and exemplify the humility code of putting the needs of the team ahead of individual success. And through galvanized collaboration they achieved their ultimate goal.

Doug demonstrated each of the six habits highlighted in this book. However, it is his humility that makes him really stand out. For most leaders, leadership is done without the glare of the spotlight. They go about their business with lots of time to reflect on their actions. Mistakes can be made and learned from in relative obscurity. Leaders of professional sports teams that compete at the highest level have a very different reality.

Every decision they make, every action they take, and every result they achieve is scrutinized by millions of people, all of whom have an opinion.

Many leaders in this realm become consumed by the power they wield. They take on a god complex where they begin to see themselves as infallible. But Doug is different. Doug has embraced a personal humility that ensures he will never be consumed by the limelight nor, as we often say, fall victim to believing his own press.

As an assistant general manager with the Dallas Stars and later as the general manager of the St. Louis Blues, Doug believed that he needed to make himself irrelevant. In his words, "You need to look outside of what you need and think about what everyone else needs. As you move up the food chain, this sacrifice must get greater and greater. My goal is to get everyone to feel good about themselves and make them feel part of what we are trying to accomplish. Great leaders are not hung up on accomplishments. Rather, they bring the right people around them to make themselves irrelevant."[1]

At the core of personal humility is the profound belief that you cannot be successful on your own. Success will come only if those around you are performing at the highest possible level, and if you share the conviction to collaborate to achieve a common goal.

It is one thing to recognize that you cannot be successful on your own. It is quite another to demonstrate humility through your actions. Don Davis and his collaborators in an article published in the *Journal of Positive Psychology* identify two components critical to success in the workplace:

1. Leaders must have insight about the limits of their knowledge, marked by openness to new ideas.

2. Leaders can regulate intellectual arrogance, marked by the ability to present their ideas in a nondefensive way and receive contrary ideas without taking offense, even when confronted with alternative viewpoints.[2]

These two tenets sit at the heart of humility in a business context. And they are not easy to enact. A norm we have seen in the corporate environment is that leaders see their role as directing the creation and implementation of strategy and supervising individuals and teams. This thinking of leadership needs to be rewired if we are to recognize the benefits of humble leadership. The thinking must change to recognize that leadership is all about the mobilization of people and that strategy must be created and implemented *through* people. Then, they must accept that there are limitations to their knowledge. Finally, they must accept that ownership of a solution requires individual involvement in the creation of the solution. Mastering the craft of sharing ideas without being directive, while allowing teams to choose their path forward, is key.

Set Ego Aside

Despite the tangible benefits of humble leadership, many leaders still have difficulty being humble. The image of a "successful" leader has been tarnished by those who have risen to the top by standing on the shoulders of others. Bill Taylor, cofounder of *Fast Company*, in a 2018 *Harvard Business Review* article, poses this exact question: "If humility is so important, why are leaders so arrogant?"[3] Taylor goes on to assert that ego and ambition often get in the way of humility. Leaders become so focused on the goal that they disregard the power of a team to help them get there. It is not hard to see where thinking like this leads to. Attention shifts to metrics, and people become little more than a means to an end. We have seen this situation play out on many occasions, and the consequences can be dire. Gradually people become disengaged. Disengagement leads to discontent. Discontent can lead to resistance as a moral and strategic stance against perceived undue or uncaring authority. And when adversity strikes—as it inevitably will—the leader is left standing alone.

Great leaders recognize that only through leveraging the skills and passions of those around them will they be able to achieve their goals. It is the leader's job to ensure each team member is engaged, has bought into the vision, and is clear on their role. This is the ideal state of humility in a leader: a conscious realization of one's own imperfect knowledge, and an understanding and acceptance of the value of others, which leads to setting high aspirations for the team.

Jim Collins spelled this out well in his book *Good to Great.* He notes that every good-to-great company he studied was led by a leader that was both ambitious and humble. He describes these leaders as "often self-effacing, quiet, reserved, and even shy," and inspired more through their own standards and ambition than through a charismatic or large personality.[4]

A leader who recognizes the power of the team and has the ambition to reach the common goal can inspire that same ambition in the team they are leading, just as Armstrong did. A leader who can inspire ambition in their team, and then empower that team to take ownership of direction and action, will see great success.

Just as leadership is about empowerment and not control, humble leadership is about the pursuit of growth, not credit. We know that success will come only from those teams who truly act in the best interest of the aligned objective. A humble leader enables that to happen.

But as we mentioned, mistakes will get made. It is the leader's job to ensure that the consequence of any mistake is a learning opportunity that will, inevitably, provide growth.

Learn from Mistakes

When a team experiences a win, it will be important for the leader to help the team understand their emotional state (e.g., pride) and their actions that led to that success. In contrast, when a team experiences a failure (which will happen), the leader must help the team acknowledge *that* emotional state (e.g., shame) as well as help individual team members learn from the failure and apply their knowledge going forward—as opposed to falling into the trap of destructive self-abasement. Mr. Busch did this for me. (I shared this story earlier, in chapter 3.) He wore the shame of my mistake. Yet he did not let that change his approach to humble leadership. He allowed me to learn and grow from the mistake I made.

Develop Humility

Humble leadership is hard work. And it is also rewarding. I recently met with the senior vice president of a large industrial organization. He was unusually buoyant. On the call, he could not wait to share the efforts and accomplishments of his team. "Mike," he said, "I'm so proud of how far they have come." He went on to talk about how three of his direct reports had taken on reach assignments, and how each of them had risen to the challenge. More than that, he was able to pinpoint where they struggled and how they were able to overcome the challenges. This was a leader who was demonstrating leadership humility. The results of his business unit are driving the transformation of his company, and the business unit's results are being driven by his humility.

For most leaders who we have met, practicing leadership humility is the most difficult of the habits to embrace. And yet the actions and beliefs that define humility can be developed and made habitual. For the many leaders for whom humility is not a natural state of being, you might wish to consider the following:

1. Establish a humility mindset. Tell yourself every day that your role is to enable others to be at their best. Recognize this as your primary accountability.

2. Carve out a minimum of one hour per week with each of your direct reports and let them set the agenda. Help them create a career plan and a development plan. Ensure this plan is connected to what matters most to them. Spend the time it takes to understand their purpose. Once you are clear on the fire that burns inside of a person, you will find it almost impossible to ignore, and you will increasingly be inclined to channel your energies to help them realize their potential.

3. Start your sentences with "We" and "They." Doing so sends the signal that you are in this together.

4. Be patient. Everyone learns at a different pace. Provided people are effective in their roles and growing, allow them the time they need to progress.

HABITUAL HUMILITY

"Ellen" was the CEO of a distribution company with over a thousand employees. She had led a strategic renewal through the global pandemic that was incredibly successful. Her industry was in turmoil, and yet her organization saw financial results *and* morale grow. But in conversation after conversation, Ellen had shown limited, if any, joy. She shrugged off the accomplishments of her company under her stewardship as trivial.

Ellen agreed to develop an individual development plan. Initially, she saw this as a task, perhaps even a burden. Academically, she was convinced it was the right thing to do, but she was not emotionally committed. In creating this plan, we explored the constructs of motivation and then went further into the habits of resilient leaders. And this is when things changed. I asked Ellen two of the questions we use at Ignite to help leaders connect with their motivating purpose (see chapter 2): "What do you want, and what do you want most?"

"I don't know," she began. She shared that she had a strong and happy marriage, and a good relationship with her children. She recognized the significant time she spends in the outdoors and that she was in excellent physical health. She reflected on the importance of financial security. She had all the money she could ever need.

Seemingly, Ellen had it all. But there was a problem. For someone who seemed to have it all, she was discontent.

And then she dropped the bomb. "I want psychological freedom," she said.

As a child, Ellen had been uprooted frequently. She was rarely in a town long enough to form the great bonds of friendship that are so deeply enriching. When she did form these bonds, her family would move shortly thereafter and the friendships would come to a halt. As the years went on, she became increasingly insular, and forming friendships seemed almost pointless.

Ellen had many professional relationships. But, like her childhood friendships, these were fleeting. She was able to identify that what she meant by "psychological freedom" was the deep bond of care-based relationships that extended beyond her family.

The floodgates had opened, and Ellen explained some of her behaviors as a leader: She used humor and sarcasm to deflect. She would withhold her true feelings rather than risk conflict or discomfort. She saw people as assets to be deployed and her role as optimizing those assets. She then asked herself, "Do I use people, or do I care for them?"

Our hope in every leadership engagement is that our client will have the willingness and motivation to change. Ellen was demonstrating both. This allowed us to dive into the leadership habits. She identified humility as the habit she wished to form.

Ellen now has a detailed plan to work on her humble leadership. "I want to move from someone who looks at people with a 'What have you done for me lately?' mindset to one who demonstrates, through her actions, that 'we are in this together,'" she said. "Because, if we can't be, the journey will be meaningless." She went on to define her purpose: "To enable my team to be podium finishers in life."

And it is our hope that she will form a few deep bonds along the way.

THE IMPORTANCE OF humility cannot be overstated. Leaders must approach humility with a sense of duty and must accept that they do not have all the requisite knowledge needed to succeed, but that the communities of interested others might. In the service of sound decision making for the greater good, leaders have a duty to find this out. Practicing humility also reminds leaders that they have an obligation to honor the value of others by inviting them to enter the conversation with all their resourcefulness, creative powers, lived experience, and energy. In this sense, demonstrated humility places sobering demands upon those who come within its reach. Ellen's story is a terrific reminder that without humility, we fight our battles alone.

SIX

OPTIMISM

MIKE

Optimism is the faith that leads to achievement.
Nothing can be done without hope and confidence.

HELEN KELLER

JOHN HERDMAN is the coach of Canada Soccer's Men's National Team. Before taking on this role, he was the leader of the Women's National Team. The latter squad had enjoyed great success with Herdman as their guide, capturing back-to-back Olympic podium finishes in 2012 and 2016. A core group of women had established themselves as leaders, and there was a young group following that included the leaders of the future. Star players like Christine Sinclair, Erin McLeod, Diana Matheson, and Kadeisha Buchanan had established themselves as household names under Herdman's stewardship.

In the words of Doug Armstrong, John had made himself irrelevant. It was time for him, at the request of Canada Soccer, to move on to the next challenge. In early 2017, he was asked to shift over to coach the Men's National Team.

This group had not been enjoying success. Although some brilliant young talent was in the pipeline, the group ranked ninety-fifth in the world.

From 2017 to 2019, the squad demonstrated continuous improvement and, when they entered the Concacaf Gold Cup in the summer of 2019, had improved their world ranking to seventy-eighth. The squad had high hopes for this tournament. A podium finish would ensure much-needed program funding and would significantly enhance their opportunity to qualify for the 2022 World Cup in Qatar.

And, to the Canadians' credit, the tournament was progressing according to Herdman's script. They had shown well in the preliminary round and had positioned themselves to play a beatable team in the quarter final, Haiti. And, again, the script was working. Well into the first half, Canada had a two-goal lead. In soccer terms, this would have appeared a near insurmountable lead. Except it wasn't. A mistake by a young Canadian defender led to Haiti scoring its first goal. This rattled the team, and twenty minutes later, a second error led to a tying goal. Things did not get better. Canada lost the game 3-2.

It was a devastating loss in a devastating fashion. Program funding and the hopes of qualifying for Qatar had depended on a podium finish. Fingers of blame were pointed, and many started to question if Herdman was the right coach for the team.

It would have been easy for Canada Soccer to have reacted hastily in these circumstances. High-caliber young players would soon be joining the squad, and World Cup matches would be played on Canadian soil in 2026. Canada Soccer could have easily justified a coaching change. However, its leaders chose to stand by Herdman. They chose patience. They chose to see if this coach and his players had more to give.

Meanwhile, Herdman was summoning his inner humility and was helping his squad get past the loss. He asked his players to assess what they learned from the loss that would enable them to become a better team.

And as is often the case in life, another opportunity presented itself. This one came for the Canadian side in the form of a friendly match against the United States on October 15, 2019. A victory in that match would keep the faint hope of qualifying for Qatar alive.

To say the stakes were high is an understatement. Canada was a heavy underdog to the United States, which was ranked more than forty-five places above the Canadians in world rankings. The American squad had ten times the number of players to choose from, and their program funding was much greater than Canada's. For a little history, the last time Canada had beaten the United States was April 1985!

Herdman invited me to that camp, and it was there that I saw firsthand what true leadership optimism is: the belief that the group will overcome whatever obstacles stand in their way; that they will succeed in their pursuit of their common purpose.

Visual representations of this purpose were everywhere. This was about playing for the Canadian flag. It was about playing to encourage young boys to embrace the sport. It was about showcasing the multicultural gift that Canada has. And it was about building a mindset of optimism. The coaching staff worked with the team to explore the concept of an indomitable spirit. They pondered people like Mohandas Gandhi, Winston Churchill, and Martin Luther King Jr.—all leaders who had faced significant adversity but who never gave up on their dream.

Before the game began, every player shared the same vision. A vision far bigger than the match itself; a vision linked to the future of the sport in Canada, and how sport can unite a nation and break down cultural barriers. Soccer may have been the vehicle, but this was about Canada.

Each player recognized the challenge they faced, and each was clear on his role. In the minutes following the opening kickoff, Canada was under a barrage. The Americans were technically skilled and a dominant force. Wave after wave crashed on the defensive corps. Yet they remained steadfast. And, in the sixty-third minute, the young superstar Alphonso Davies broke free and opened the scoring for Canada. It was a euphoric moment, but it was not time to rest. The Americans pressed harder, throwing all the talent and experience they had at this young squad. It was a game for the ages. And, as they approached the final seconds of the match, Canadian stalwart Lucas Cavallini scored the side's second goal to seal the match. Hopes for Qatar were alive. Victory was sweet.

Many things had to go right for Canada on that day. None more than the players keeping their indomitable spirit and belief that they would succeed.

Unlike with sports, real life rarely comes down to do-or-die moments. But adversity will come. Businesses will be disrupted. Situations will threaten to take people off track. It is a defined purpose supported by an indomitable will and the belief that the shared goal is worth the sacrifice and effort that enables organizations to be resilient and persevere.

We saw this in chapter 1 in how Terry handled the COVID-19 crisis of 2020. His business was facing a crisis unlike anything it had seen before. Yet he believed from the onset of the pandemic that the crisis would end and, if he and his team did the right things, the company would emerge stronger than they had ever been. Terry embraced adversity as opportunity and, with steadfast belief, focused on what needed to be done to ensure both short-term and long-term success.

His staff picked up on these signals. It impacted their confidence. And it changed their approach. Terry's team proceeded with unwavering belief.

The stories of Herdman and Terry serve as examples of the impact optimism can have when we are facing adversity.

Simply put, optimism is a mindset that has one anticipating the good, as opposed to anticipating the bad. Either will have a substantial impact on one's life. A sense of optimism can fuel innovation, build resilience, and motivate you to persevere through the toughest of times. Leaders who fear the worst will be more prone to accepting mediocrity. Their mindset permeates their team, who invariably embrace negativity, which stifles creativity. People become reactive and, instead of thinking "What might we do?," they embrace the thought "Here's why we can't..."

For business leaders, it is important to understand both how critical it is to demonstrate optimism from the top down and to apply the habit in a way that is purposeful and actionable. Employees who rally behind their leadership team are the ones who can see their leaders demonstrating optimism to overcome the toughest obstacles and thrive. So, just what is required for optimistic leadership?

Avoid Arbitrariness

We see in leaders two approaches to optimism. One is very healthy. The other can lead to ruin. These might be best explained by looking at the Stockdale Paradox.

James Stockdale, former vice-presidential candidate, naval officer, and Vietnam prisoner of war, is well known for his views on optimism based on his personal experience. He explained to Jim Collins, author of *Good to Great*, the unwavering optimism he had during his time as a POW, when he never doubted that he would be freed in the end. He was also optimistic in seeing how his time as a POW would eventually serve as a valuable life experience for him.

However, one of the biggest takeaways from the discussion for Collins was the paradoxical approach in which Stockdale positioned his unwavering belief that he would be freed. When Collins asked him who didn't make it out of the POW camp, Stockdale gave a surprising answer. "Oh, that's easy," he told Collins. "The optimists."[1]

Stockdale went on to explain that the optimists were the ones who placed arbitrary timelines—timelines of blind hope—on their release. They figured they'd be out by Christmas. And when Christmas passed, they figured on Easter. Then on Thanksgiving, and so on and so forth. Stockdale's take was that the optimists "died of a broken heart."[2]

The Stockdale Paradox is, then, about the difference between blind optimism ("We'll be out by Christmas") and purposeful optimism. Purposeful optimism—shared by Herdman, Terry, and Stockdale—dictates that one cannot afford to lose faith, and, equally important, one must confront the brutal truth of a situation and take aligned actions in pursuit of desired outcomes. Blind optimism—one without action or discipline—does not yield any results and can be devastating (to the point of death, as Stockdale notes).

Leaders need to see the distinction in the two approaches and allow that to guide how they work with their teams. Leaders who are overly driven by dates and specific achievements can crush the spirit of their people, whereas those who help implant a deep and passionate purpose that makes the effort worthwhile will set up their teams for greatness.

In our strategic planning work with companies, we often call on learnings from John F. Kennedy, a truly indomitable spirit. In group sessions with leadership teams, we often play a video of Kennedy's speech at Rice University where he shares with a nation that "we choose to go to the moon. We choose to go to the moon... and do the other things, not because they are easy, but because they are hard."[3] We then have participants dissect his speech. Invariably, teams recognize that he was putting a proverbial stake in the ground. They recognize that this pursuit was purpose driven. America was in the middle of the Cold War. People were frightened. The Soviets had beaten America to orbit. Nuclear war was a real threat. America needed hope. Participants also point out that in this speech, Kennedy demonstrates his belief that going to the moon was achievable by calling out what needed to be done right and what could go wrong. Under the blazing Texas sun, he had convinced a nation to join him on a pursuit. One which was noble, and one the nation became convinced it would achieve.

The point of the exercise is to demonstrate to leaders the importance of being clear on their vision and sharing it with the people around them. It is also to demonstrate the importance for leaders to connect to the people around them in terms that matter to those people. And finally, it is so they can recognize that the pursuit will be hard and success will depend on confronting challenges and building plans that will help overcome the inherent obstacles they will face.

Smile

When I was growing up, my mother saw in me something I didn't see in myself. She saw that I was a brooder. I would spend time worrying about the trivial and the serious, and she understood this wasn't a particularly healthy habit. With a smile and a look, she would convey the message "It's going to be okay. You can do it."

I would love to say that this was enough. But I needed a more regular reminder. As I hit my teens, mom came home one day with a small poster. She asked me to put it up on the wall of my bedroom between those of the wide range of musicians and athletes I admired. It carried a simple message from an unknown author: "We worry as though we had a thousand years to live. Let us, rather, strive for the gentle humor of the heart that knows how to smile at the world."

In my case, the adage is true: Moms know best. I've never forgotten the simple message of that poster. We will face challenging times in our lives. Sometimes things will feel catastrophic. But if we can pause and take in a deep breath, exhale, and smile, we will often realize that things are not nearly as bad as they might seem.

The urge to brush aside a simple smile as being corny or trite is strong. But the science is undeniable. A smile conveys a message to all around us: "People who smile express positive social intentions that are essential for the creation and maintenance of social bonds."[4] A smile to our colleagues says things are going to be all right: "A happy face signals positive emotions, as well as attachment, availability, care, support, and credibility."[5] When the smile comes from a leader, it is felt by an entire team. The smile instills confidence. Confidence breeds resiliency.

Larry Stefan, an industrial psychologist based in Vancouver, shares the following about the importance of joy in leadership.

"People naturally enjoy working with someone who is joyful," he says. "Joyful leaders act like a magnet attracting people to them. Their attitude and approach to things tends to relax those around them and encourages input. Contrast this with a serious and dour type of leader. People unconsciously almost try to avoid dealing with such a person and are fearful of making errors and being reprimanded."[6]

Dr. Stefan's words link directly back to the concept of resilience. Joyful leaders will be less intimidating to their colleagues and more welcoming to new ideas, and their joyfulness will subconsciously encourage colleagues to embrace the leader's positive vibes.

How to Embrace Optimistic Leadership

Optimism is an attribute that defines us. Life will deal us many setbacks if we choose to truly live it. Those who believe they will prevail in their darkest hours have mastered optimism. Those who think in terms of worst-case scenarios and the fear of what *might* happen are destined to be reactive in times of change.

The stereotypical view of an optimist is that they are a passive person who believes that if they think good thoughts, good things will happen. That is *not* what an optimist is. That is a "blind optimist." True optimists take the time to seek knowledge, to understand their landscape, to assess their areas of risk, and to take appropriate action in pursuit of their desired outcomes. What makes them optimists is that they believe that, by taking these actions, they *will* achieve their desired results.

Demonstrating and cultivating a sense of optimism in a team is critical to organizational success. We don't even need to have optimism embedded in our DNA to do it. Any leader can foster a sense of optimism by following some straightforward steps:

- Build a compelling, purpose-driven view of the future.
  - > Work with your senior leaders to understand what drives them.
  - > Construct a vision that aligns the purpose of your organization with an envisioned end state.
  - > Allow people the time and space to understand the vision and translate their day-to-day activities to the pursuit.

- Confront reality.
  - > Engage your team to understand what might go wrong.
  - > Be clear on what is standing in your way.
  - > Identify the compelling organizational gifts that give you the belief that you will succeed.

- Identify a clear road map.
  - > Remember that Kennedy was able to mobilize a nation by calling out the things it would need to get right if it were to put a person on the moon.

- Embrace discomfort.
  - > Accept before you make changes in order to adapt to a new landscape that mistakes will happen. Establish a mindset that the setbacks are necessary to achieve ultimate success.

- Be unwavering.
  - > Bring important conversations back to your vision. When facing a setback, ask the team if they are still aligned with the ultimate pursuit. This simple question will reorient thinking.

WHEN I WORK with leaders, I often ask them to picture themselves in retirement, feeling that they had accomplished what they had set out to accomplish in life. I ask them to share how they will be feeling in that future state. Then I ask them what they see happening around them. And, lastly, I ask them to articulate what accomplishments have enabled them to be in this place.

The point of the exercise is to help them establish true purpose and to explore the path they must embark on in pursuit of that purpose. And then, most importantly, I ask them what choices they are willing to make *now* in the service of that pursuit. Then we reflect again on that future state. This serves as a navigational beacon to keep them optimistically on track.

It should be no different at the enterprise level. If we accept that strategy is achieved through people, we create a vision that is aligned with the collective's individual purpose; if we choose to embrace discomfort and be unwavering in the face of it, we will be demonstrating the habit of optimism and enhancing the resilience of our team.

SEVEN

COURAGE

ALI

*Courage is not the absence of fear, but rather
the assessment that something else is
more important than fear.*

FRANKLIN D. ROOSEVELT

T IGNITE, we witness two distinct forms of courage: the courage of one's convictions (or leading with principles in the face of opposition or adversity), and the courage to be uncomfortable (or acting despite the fear of discomfort and failure).

The courage of one's convictions is rarely called upon, but critical. It is required when a leader's values or principles conflict with a decision or action; these are critical decision-making moments that many leaders describe as crucible moments in their careers.

Tamara Vrooman is one such leader. In 2008, when the global financial crisis threw millions out of work, forced home-owners into foreclosure, caused huge financial institutions to collapse, and siphoned tax dollars out of the economy and into massive government bailout efforts, Tamara was acting as the newly appointed CEO of a well-known credit union, Vancity.

Like many institutions, Vancity's profits had plummeted—in this case, nearly 40 percent from the previous year. Without a doubt, Tamara's appointment as CEO had come at a time of severe scrutiny.

Tamara and the board of directors addressed the crisis head-on and tackled internal challenges first, streamlining leadership, cutting costs, and optimizing cash flow. They also decided to increase its interest rates on their mortgage-secured credit facilities. Not surprisingly, this was met with fierce pushback from members who were already suffering the effects of the crisis: as members of a values-based and community-oriented credit union, they felt betrayed.

The board and executive team felt that hiking interest rates was necessary for the survival of the institution; they also reasoned that they'd likely not lose many clients, as there were few alternatives. For those clients, the cost of switching institutions would be far greater than the cost of the proposed rate increase. As such, Tamara was initially supportive of the raise. But it did not sit quite right with her. She knew that they had made an agreement with the members, and they were now making unilateral changes to that agreement.

The initial rollout was a success. There was pushback, but most members were signing off on the rate increase. However, the unease that Tamara initially felt continued to fester. The comments made by those who complained resonated with her. She realized that the decision was inconsistent with her values. And, once she realized this, the path forward became clear. She needed to reverse the decision.

Like most critical leadership decisions, Tamara's was difficult to execute. An executive team and board had fully endorsed the rate hike. She would be overriding her executive and not asking, but rather telling, the board that the path needed to change.

This story epitomizes courage of conviction. Only the board and Tamara are privy to what Tamara said that convinced the board to reverse the decision. However, I suspect that she was honest about her feelings and expressed remorse in following the decision rather than sticking to her values. To the board, I suspect the underlying message was "If we do not reverse this decision, I am not the right leader for this organization."

Tamara saw her actions with the board as one of the defining moments in her career. It was the moment when she knew she needed to trust her instincts and be guided by her values in everything she does.

Tamara has been credited with transforming Vancity's business model. It was, at one time, another financial institution in a crowded landscape. By putting the needs of community and individual members ahead of corporate interests, Tamara put Vancity on the course to becoming a globally renowned leader in values-based banking.

In 2020, the COVID-19 crisis created an opportunity for defining moments for many leaders around the world, including Terry.

Terry was clear on his purpose: to continue his family's legacy of a company that cared about the well-being of people and the community. The decisions that were required during the pandemic were painful. He knew the impact they would have on people's lives, and he struggled over them. And he had the courage to tell his organization openly and transparently what he was going to do and why he was going to do it. He did this through town halls and email. He invited one-on-one communication with impacted employees, and he spoke the truth.

Terry knew that many would not be happy with his decisions. But he stood by those decisions. They were what was required to ensure the sustainability of the business. The response from his employees shocked him. He was delivering some of the worst news many of these people had ever heard and was expecting strong backlash. Their jobs were being terminated at a time when the prospects for new employment were bleaker than ever. Yet the majority of people Terry spoke with indicated that they understood his reasons and decisions.

Terry's actions during the pandemic were not unlike those of many senior leaders. Making sound business decisions does not take a lot of courage. But doing so transparently and taking ownership of the decisions does. His convictions were clear, he had the courage to act on them, and he communicated his decisions in a way that demonstrated compassion and care for his employees.

Courage of one's convictions, as expressed by Tamara and Terry, requires integrity, born from a strong sense of self and purpose, as well as a strong moral compass. It means, simply, doing the right thing. "From caring comes courage,"[1] said the ancient Chinese philosopher Lao-tzu. If we are clear on what matters, we will find courage.

The second form of courage is the courage to be uncomfortable. This courage is called upon regularly. It is the courage to deliver tough feedback because you know your team members will need it to grow. It is the courage to trust your team with important work because you know you can't do it alone. It is the courage to stretch your skills and abilities or lead your team into uncharted waters because you know you must in order to reach greater heights.

In the mid-1990s, I was learning volleyball in gym class. I couldn't get the hang of the overhand serve and I felt frustrated.

I was good at the underhand serve, and I didn't understand why I had to learn to do it a different way. Consciously or not, I was afraid of embarrassing myself. While I may have lacked courage, I had no shortage of work ethic. I practiced morning and night with my dad in the front yard. "I can't do it!" I would wail. He'd calmly respond, "You can't do it *yet*." I never mastered the skill, but I did become competent enough to not humiliate myself in gym class.

Why are we so afraid of failure and judgment? Thomas DeLong's book *Flying without a Net* is a useful resource for leaders who want to move past their fear and draw strength from vulnerability. In it, DeLong presents the powerful construct of having courage to "do the right things poorly" before "doing the right things well."[2] This idea stems from the conscious competence model of learning a new skill, developed in the 1970s by education consultant Noel Burch. Burch posited that we move through several stages of learning before a new skill becomes natural or automatic.[3] It takes courage to do something when we are "consciously unskilled," as I was with the overhand serve.

Building Courage

Albert Einstein, in a letter to his son, wrote, "It is the same with people as it is with riding a bike. Only when moving can one comfortably maintain one's balance."[4] And it is the same with organizations as it is with people. We must keep moving, growing, and changing. This is one reason so many once-successful organizations become complacent and ultimately begin to decline. It is also one reason many individuals reach a point in their lives where they settle (often into the couch) and stop moving. They grow comfortable with the way things are and don't have the courage to change.

We are hardwired to avoid loss, and if we're comfortable, that means there is something to lose. The cognitive bias of "loss aversion" was first identified by psychologists Amos Tversky and Daniel Kahneman in 1979, in the context of economics, to explain why the pain of losing is psychologically more powerful than the prospect of gaining something equivalent.[5] Over the next decade, psychologists identified several related (but distinct) decision-making tendencies toward retaining the status quo, including what's known as "status quo bias" and "psychological inertia."[6] There is a lack of consensus on whether these tendencies are evolutionary in nature, but there is ample evidence that they are common. Sir Isaac Newton's law of inertia gives us an apt analogy for our tendency to retain the status quo: "If a body is at rest or moving at a constant speed in a straight line, it will remain at rest or keep moving in a straight line at constant speed unless it is acted upon by a force."[7] It is the same with people. It takes incredible force to change our course or push ourselves to grow. And it is, quite naturally, uncomfortable. However, there is no growth without discomfort.

My courage to do things that make me uncomfortable has grown since high-school gym class, but, like a muscle, I had to actively stress it for it to grow.

In spring 2017, I was preparing to leave for basic military officer training, and I was nervous. I whined to my partner, Jamie, "What if I can't keep up? What will happen if I can't do enough push-ups?" I was afraid of the unknown and afraid I wasn't strong enough. Three months later, I graduated top of my class. My courage grew significantly from that experience.

I learned that my fears were out of proportion with reality. And I learned that I can do hard things.

Courage isn't reckless. It's a deliberate, disciplined process. Kathleen Reardon, professor emerita at the University of Southern California's Marshall School of Business, defines courage as a special kind of calculated risk taking. She says,

> People who become good leaders have a greater than average willingness to make bold moves, but they strengthen their chances of success—and avoid career suicide—through careful deliberation and preparation. Business courage is not so much a visionary leader's inborn characteristic as a skill acquired through decision-making processes that improve with practice. In other words, most great business leaders teach themselves to make high-risk decisions. They learn to do this well over time, often decades.[8]

Courage is learned through the experience of risk taking. And even the smallest of steps build our courage. A few years ago, I wanted to take a Krav Maga fighting class, but I was afraid of looking bad. I signed up anyway and survived. It is these small acts of courage that build our strength.

Practice stepping out of your comfort zone; take small steps to build your courage over time. It can also be useful, when fearful, to consider the worst-case scenario. When clients are weighing a decision, I often ask, "What's the worst that could happen?" Typically, they realize that the worst case is both unlikely and not that scary. And when the stakes are high, understanding the worst-case scenario allows them to create a contingency plan, which creates comfort when moving forward.

Growing courage of one's convictions is more complex. You must first get in touch with your purpose, as we discussed earlier in this book, and with your values. You must consider what it means to you to live and lead with integrity. What are the values or principles with which you choose to live? These answers will support you in the defining moments of your life.

Like every habit of resilient leaders, courage both supports and is a result of the other habits and of resiliency in general. "Courage is the enforcing virtue," said Senator John McCain, "the one that makes possible all the other virtues common to exceptional leaders: honesty, integrity, confidence, compassion, and humility."[9] Resilient leaders are more courageous because they have a strong sense of self and a strong team behind them. And practicing courage makes us more resilient. Resilient leaders don't cave into themselves when things get tough. They take themselves through a disciplined process of decision making, guided by purpose and values, with trust in their teams, and move forward despite their fear.

EIGHT

DISCIPLINE

ALI

No man is free who is not master of himself.

EPICTETUS

WALTER MISCHEL, the late psychologist who laid the foundation for decades of research on self-control and life outcomes, said,

> Self-control is crucial for the successful pursuit of long-term goals. It is equally essential for developing the self-restraint and empathy needed to build caring and mutually supportive relationships. It can help people avoid becoming impervious to consequences or getting stuck in jobs they hate. It is the "master aptitude" underlying emotional intelligence, essential for constructing a fulfilling life.[1]

Mischel is talking, in other words, about discipline—the "master aptitude" that bridges the gap between a desire to change and results. It is the habit of resilient leaders that enables action and growth. In a leadership context, discipline is multilayered, ranging from the practice of self-care, to how leaders "show up" or self-regulate, to how leaders engage in strategic thinking, to how leaders manage others to achieve results. And self-discipline is the "master" habit that enables leaders to sustain behavior change across all six habits.

Self-Care

Discipline is the single most important habit for managing one's health, time, and energy. The most resilient leaders are those who are unrelenting in their efforts to prioritize their health and use their time well: they prioritize diet, exercise, and sleep; they identify and focus on only those activities that are the best use of their time; and they understand what they must do to manage their energy on a daily, weekly, and monthly basis, such as taking regular breaks throughout the day, scheduling uninterrupted thinking time every week, and taking time off.

From a young age, I planned my days and kept track of what had to be done. I scheduled everything in, not just for the evening of homework but also at the end of the week and for projects coming due in the future. I kept a journal where I plotted the times I was to begin my tasks. I would even schedule phone calls with my friends. I still operate this way today, establishing priorities, identifying the things that need to be done and the time needed to do them, and scheduling time in my calendar for exercise, eating lunch, taking a walk, reviewing reports, and preparing for meetings. This discipline is one way in which I ensure I make time for the things that matter.

DISCIPLINE IMBALANCE

I recently helped a senior leader, "Darrian," develop an individual leadership development plan. His firm's managing partner held Darrian's talent in high esteem, but the partner also lamented that Darrian had no life outside of work, and because of that, no one wanted to work with him because of the stress he put on himself and on others. In our sessions, Darrian identified discipline as one of his strongest habits; however, he was exhibiting a complete lack of discipline in managing his stress levels and prioritizing his personal life. He shared that he hadn't taken a vacation in years and worked nonstop. Ironically, he was incredibly disciplined in his management of projects, and the quality of his work was exceptional, but his job was at risk because his stress levels and lack of balance were impacting how he showed up with his supervisor, peers, and direct reports. Over a few weeks of working together, Darrian came to realize that self-care, or work-life balance, or whatever one chooses to call it, is not an indulgence, it's a necessary aspect of being a resilient leader.

This ability to manage one's health, time, and energy also directly impacts the next layer of discipline: discipline in how a leader chooses to show up.

Self-Regulation

In an article summarizing their book *The Power of Resilience*, Drs. Robert Brooks and Sam Goldstein identify discipline as critical to developing a resilient mindset.

Self-discipline and self-control play a significant role in our daily activities. When we think before we act, when we consider the feelings of others, when we reflect upon possible solutions to problems, when we behave in a rational and thoughtful way, when we engage in developing a business plan, when we keep from screaming at someone who has done something to make us angry, we are displaying self-discipline and self-control.

Self-regulation, they say, "is a major component of resilience."[2] Brooks and Goldstein emphasize the cognitive aspects of discipline here, but the ability to regulate the nervous system is also critical, hence the importance of doing nervous system-regulating practices such as yoga, tai chi, and mindfulness.

Mischel, when asked to summarize the fundamental message from research on self-control, recalled Descartes's famous "I think, therefore I am." He said,

What has been discovered about mind, brain, and self-control lets us move from his proposition to "I think, therefore I can change what I am." Because by changing how we think, we can change what we feel, do, and become. If that leads to the question "But can I really change?" I reply with what George Kelly said to his therapy clients when they kept asking him if they could get control of their lives. He looked straight into their eyes and said, "Would you like to?"[3]

Management Discipline

Resilient leaders practice discipline in managing their teams in the pursuit of organizational results. A distinction is often made between management and leadership, with a call for leaders to be leaders and not managers. But this is an unhelpful distinction. A resilient leader must be both. Leaders must exercise discipline in establishing what needs to be done and in holding people accountable for both action and results.

In *Good to Great*, Jim Collins's research underscores the powerful, differentiating role of discipline. The companies that made the leap from good to great got the right people on the team ("disciplined people"), engaged them to ask and answer the right strategic questions ("disciplined thought"), and held themselves and others accountable to the strategy with unyielding discipline and accountability ("disciplined action"). This last element—accountability—is essential for organizational discipline. With the right people on the team and the right strategy, the necessary foundation is in place, but the leader must still be disciplined in creating accountability for adherence to strategy and standards and achieving results.

I have worked with several CEOs who lamented the lack of accountability among their executive teams. It is always a difficult shift for them to see that if there is a lack of accountability in the culture, it is because they have not been holding people accountable, and that without consequences there is no accountability. Resilient leaders have the inner discipline to hold themselves accountable, which makes it easier to hold others accountable.

Discipline Killers

There are many reasons a person might lack discipline. A person's upbringing or personality traits may play a role. In the case of management discipline, a lack of confidence or desire to be liked may stand in the way of setting clear expectations or holding others accountable. And a desire to please may make it difficult for someone to decline invitations or requests, resulting in an overflowing and unmanageable life. Our environment is a factor, with the internet and social media impacting leaders' ability to concentrate, focus, and exercise restraint.[4] And certain mental health challenges can also deplete a person's willpower. We cannot address all the potential discipline killers in this book. But you can act by considering what is hindering your discipline, and then work to address the root causes.

If you find your motivation fades by the afternoon, do your most important work in the morning. If you don't get up to exercise because you don't sleep well, identify what is disrupting your sleep. Consider looking at your efforts to instill discipline as a game or experiment, in pursuit of a system that works for you. Because what works for one person may not work for another. And it is up to each of us to identify the obstacles, eliminate them wherever possible, and build processes that work for our unique natures and circumstances.

One Habit to Rule Them All

The intent of Ignite's leadership development work is not only to help leaders understand what good looks like but also to make the six habits sticky; that is, to create conditions that increase the likelihood that individuals will practice the habits consistently and, ultimately, sustain them. Self-discipline is key to sustained behavior change. Whether you are striving to build the fundamentals of discipline or working on the other habits of resilient leaders, the key ingredients of sustained change are a strong motivating purpose, habitual practice, and managing setbacks.

Humans are creatures of habit. Only 5 percent of our choices are consciously self-selected, whereas 95 percent of behaviors are habitual or in reaction to strong external stimuli.[5] The more that behaviors are routinized in the form of deliberate practice, the less energy they require and the more they recur automatically. It is clear from the science of habits that behavior change must be looked at as an integrated development process over time, not a one-off event.[6] As you seek to change your leadership, focus on one or two habits to start, and identify a few small, specific behaviors that relate to those habits. Create a simple action plan of when and how you will practice these behaviors; create auditory or visual cues as reminders; involve others, including peers and supervisors; and seek feedback.

If Darrian had attempted to become disciplined in self-care and work-life balance because the managing partner told him to, he would have failed. To succeed, he first had to realize that this change was critical to achieving his long-term personal vision—to have impact, achieve through others, and spend time with the people who matter most to him. Once the motivation was clear, we identified small actions or rituals he could implement consistently that would move him in the right direction.

Implementing small rituals or systems in your day-to-day life not only ensures that you do the things that matter;

it also instills a sense of discipline that will carry over to your approach to your teams and organization. In basic military officer training, soldiers are trained to build personal discipline through daily habits, such as making the bed each morning, cleaning and pressing uniforms, and keeping to a tight schedule in off-hours. These small rituals not only ensure the soldier is prepared for the unexpected but also instills in them a sense of order and responsibility that is reflected in their leadership. It is this ability to manage oneself in seemingly small ways that gives a person the discipline to change in bigger ways.

There will be times when you fall back into older, unhelpful behavior patterns. This should be expected, and so you should have a plan for when it happens. Megan Call, associate director of University of Utah Health's Resiliency Center, has found that individuals most often bounce back and forth between action, relapse, and contemplation. She notes that when a setback occurs, it is valuable to "acknowledge the lapse as part of the change process and treat the occasion as a learning opportunity." Call suggests asking yourself these questions after experiencing a setback:

- What did I learn from this setback?

- What needs to happen to get back into action?

- How do I want to treat myself while working toward change?[7]

This approach suggests that for an individual to be positioned to manage setbacks well, the process of leadership development must create a positive mindset toward setbacks; that is, setbacks should be normalized, and approached with compassion and curiosity.

As you progress through your leadership journey, encountering setbacks along the way, remember that change isn't easy, straightforward, or fast, and relapse is inevitable. Look for ways to position the change process as one of experimentation and learning, and leverage your inquisitiveness as a foundational behavior for sustained change.

CONCLUSION

MIKE

Wisdom doesn't grow on our good days.

MIKE WATSON

N 1972, Helen Reddy won the Grammy Award for Best Female Pop Vocal Performance for her song, "I Am Woman." The chorus of this song goes:

> *Oh yes, I am wise*
> *But it's wisdom born of pain*
> *Yes, I've paid the price*
> *But look how much I've gained*
> *If I have to, I can do anything...*[1]

Throughout this book, Ali and I share components of our personal journeys, including the obstacles and setbacks we faced. In my case, the setbacks represented wobbles in both character and competence. I am not proud of the mistakes that I have made. On occasion, I can still feel the rush of blood to my cheeks and the strain on my diaphragm caused by the shame I feel about some of my actions and nonactions. I take solace in the knowledge that I have owned these mistakes and use them as learning tools to make me a better person and a better leader.

At Ignite, we have yet to meet a leader who has not wobbled in their journey. What we have seen, however, is the difference in how leaders have responded to adversity. Leaders like Darrian and Anthony faltered and used their errors to become stronger. They applied the learning and they changed. Others were unable or unwilling to change. Unlike Darrian and Anthony, those leaders could not look in the mirror and accept that they were not great and that they needed to change. They could not rise up to the occasion to embrace the challenge of a difficult and transformative personal journey to become the best versions of themselves.

One engagement in particular I will always remember. We had been asked by the board of directors of a global brand to work with the CEO to help instill humanistic leadership in their vision and strategy. The problem was clear from the outset. The CEO exhibited narcissistic tendencies. He did not have a deep level of care for the people in the organization and was driven by his desire to maintain personal power. It manifested in him as a void in trust, inquisitiveness, and humility. After a few months of our efforts, it became clear that he viewed us as a necessary evil that had been prescribed by his board. He kept us at a distance. He would, however, have us review his monthly board reports before he submitted them. This was a mechanism to demonstrate to the board that we were still involved. We received monthly payments from the organization that would have been justifiable had we been involved in the activities being referenced. Instead, we were being paid an exorbitant fee for affixing our signature to a report.

I was quite attached to the fee. It was significant. But we were not fulfilling our mandate. I talked to the CEO in question and shared my concerns. His response verged on flippant: we could continue to receive this healthy retainer for our signature, or we could withdraw from the engagement.

Of course, we withdrew. We asked for and received an audience with the executive committee of the board to explain our decision. They shared that the challenge of the CEO's behavior was real, and they made a conscious decision to accept our withdrawal from the engagement and, more importantly, to accept his behavior. The CEO's brand in the public eye was more important to the committee than the challenges that arose from his behavior.

Less than a year later, the organization found itself embroiled in controversy that led straight to the desk of the CEO, who then retired. The organization had suffered a monumental blow to its credibility with the public. Less than two years later, it was sold to a third party at pennies on the dollar.

This story always brings back feelings of pain for me. This organization had a workforce of incredible, purpose-driven people. Many of them quietly left. The leader, who was a master in the space, could have helped them achieve greatness. Instead, his (and his board's) unwillingness to change led to the organization's ultimate demise. I will always view this as a personal failure.

Experiences like this were a driving force behind the writing of this book. We wanted to create a tool for leaders to understand and constructively address their deficiencies, while empowering them to build habitual practices that will translate into stronger, more resilient teams. While there is no shortage of literature on the subject, and the leaders we work with have access to this literature (and many of them are voracious consumers of it), we find that many still struggle to make the changes they initiate habitual, despite their knowing what good leadership entails.

We believe this is because enacting change is much harder than it sounds. Leadership is all about behavior. And how a leader behaves is deeply ingrained, influenced heavily by things like a person's upbringing and life experiences. To change these behaviors, a leader must have a strong desire to change and a compelling motivation for that change. It is the path of least resistance to look at others and ponder what they should be doing differently. It is far more difficult to look in the mirror and self-assess. And this is where this book stands apart from the others. Before enacting any of the essential habits of resilient leaders, you must first look in the mirror and hold yourself accountable. You must have the discipline to acknowledge your strengths and weaknesses, you must intimately understand your desire to achieve phenomenal results, and you must know that only by engaging the hearts and minds of the people you work with will you be truly successful.

And self-assessment is only the beginning.

Once you have the desire and motivation to change, you need to be specific in what you will choose to do differently. Each of us starts from a different place. There is no one-size-fits-all solution. It requires hard work to identify, with specificity, what actions and behaviors you will choose to address. Enacting a change in those behaviors is the next step, and this requires trial-and-error. It requires a third party to point out where you may be wobbling. And it requires fortitude and tenacity. Most of all, it requires that you show up, each day, ready to face your fears in a nonjudgmental way.

We are in one of the most transformational times in human history. The stresses we are under are immense. The unprecedented pace of change we are experiencing today is the slowest pace of change we will see for the rest of our lives. It is in this environment that we are asking leaders to pause and reflect on how they are showing up each day, and to change how they show up in order to become better leaders. Yet it is when under immense stress that change can be the hardest. Be aware of this as you start your journey to resiliency.

In the preface, I recognized that in my early career my teams achieved great results despite the flaws in my leadership. Some may say "Great. Then why change?" The reason is because despite achieving great results, I always felt empty. There was nothing truly gratifying in it. It was only when I embraced leadership as being about the people I served that I began to feel true satisfaction in my career and in my life.

It is our hope that through our exploration of the six habits of resilient leaders, and through the success stories of leaders who have embraced those habits, you too will be able to apply the habits in your life and find the same satisfaction in your career. Ultimately, our wish is for you to become the resilient leader that the people in your life deserve.

ACKNOWLEDGMENTS

MIKE

RISE UP needed to be rooted in human psychology. Deep thanks to one of the best humans we have ever met, Dan Stone, who tested each line to ensure consistency with his area of expertise, clinical counseling.

The decision to write a book on leadership came at an odd moment. We were enjoying a celebratory meeting with a valued client, Fraser Surrey Docks. Executives had challenged themselves to put a stake in the ground with a personal aspiration. After going around the table, the CEO, Jeff Scott—who has become a great friend—paused the conversation and asked what I was willing to commit to. I was on the spot and an inner thought was vocalized for the first time, "I will write a book." Jeff, thank you for your encouragement, friendship, and support.

We are grateful to the Ignite team. Our colleagues were always available to support with research and goodwill.

Dana Robbins ... your generosity of spirit knows no bounds. It was an honor to have such a gifted publisher and great leader help us make *Rise Up* the best it could be.

We reference many leaders in the book, and we interviewed countless others. Special thanks to those great leaders who took the time to share their insights with us, especially Doug Armstrong, Ken Holland, Tamara Vrooman, Shauneen Bruder, John Herdman, and Mike Leonard.

We started with a jumble of words on a page and finished with a book we are proud of. The Figure 1 team made this a reality, and brought great expertise, patience, and a sense of humor. Thank you.

Over the years, I've worked with wonderful people who have taught me great lessons on leadership. To all my former colleagues at TD Bank and BlueShore Financial, thank you. You gave me the space to make mistakes and grow as a leader.

Inspiration comes from many places. For me, it comes from the relationships we form along the way. None had more meaning to me than my friends through the Chamber of Commerce network. Special thanks go to Craig Hougen, Michael McMullen, David Paterson, and Perrin Beatty.

And, lastly, there are those people who lift us up when we are down. Life can be hard. And being the best versions of ourselves requires supportive family and friends. Thank you to my family, Gill, Chris, and KT, and to dear friends, Renato Cavaliere, Mike Boehm, Siavosh Moussavi, and Shelby Boehm, whom I know will always have my back.

NOTES

Chapter 1: Resilient Leadership

1 Gerd Leonhard, "Digital Transformation: Are You Ready for Exponential Change?" Vimeo, 2018, https://vimeo.com/276846809.

2 Ranjay Gulati, Nitin Nohria, and Franz Wohlgezogen, "Roaring Out of a Recession," *Harvard Business Review*, March 2010, https://hbr.org/2010/03/roaring-out-of-recession.

Chapter 2: Motivation

1 Mihaly Csikszentmihalyi, *Flow: The Psychology of Optimal Experience*, Harper & Row, 1990.

2 Daniel H. Pink, *Drive: The Surprising Truth about What Motivates Us*, Riverhead Books, 2009.

3 M.D. Butler, *The Longevity Revolution: The Benefits and Challenges of Living a Long Life*, Public Affairs Books, 2008.

4 "Quotes by Arthur Ashe," CMG Worldwide, n.d., http://www.cmgww.com/sports/ashe/quotes/.

5 Lucius Annaeus Seneca and Robin Campbell, *Letters from a Stoic: Epistulae Morales ad Lucilium*, Penguin Books, 1969.

Chapter 3: Trust

1 Kurt T. Dirks and Donald L. Ferrin, "Trust in Leadership: Meta-Analytic Findings and Implications for Research and Practice," *Journal of Applied Psychology*, 87, 4 (August 2002): 611–28, https://ink.library.smu.edu.sg/cgi/viewcontent.cgi?article=1674&context=lkcsb_research.

2 Tony Simons, "The High Cost of Lost Trust," *Harvard Business Review*, September 2002, https://hbr.org/2002/09/the-high-cost-of-lost-trust.

3   Stephen M.R. Covey and Douglas R. Conant, "The Connection between Employee Trust and Financial Performance," *Harvard Business Review*, July 18, 2016, https://hbr.org/2016/07/the-connection-between-employee-trust-and-financial-performance.
4   Shauneen Bruder, in discussion with the author, 2015.
5   Anonymous client comment, shared in session facilitated by the author, 2018.
6   Nitin Nohria, convocation address to Harvard Business School MBA class of 2019.
7   Anonymous client comment, shared in session facilitated by the author, 2016.
8   Anonymous client comment, shared in session facilitated by the author, 2019.

Chapter 4: Inquisitiveness

1   Francesca Gino, "The Business Case for Curiosity," *Harvard Business Review*, September–October 2018, https://hbr.org/2018/09/the-business-case-for-curiosity.
2   Gino, "The Business Case for Curiosity."
3   Karl Weick, "Prepare Your Organization to Fight Fires," *Harvard Business Review*, May–June 1996, https://hbr.org/1996/05/prepare-your-organization-to-fight-fires.

Chapter 5: Humility

1   Doug Armstrong, personal conversation with the author, 2016.
2   Don E. Davis et al., "Distinguishing Intellectual Humility and General Humility," *Journal of Positive Psychology* 11, 3 (2016): 215–24, https://doi.org/10.1080/17439760.2015.1048818.
3   Bill Taylor, "If Humility Is So Important, Why Are Leaders So Arrogant?" *Harvard Business Review*, October 15, 2018, https://hbr.org/2018/10/if-humility-is-so-important-why-are-leaders-so-arrogant.
4   Jim Collins, *Good to Great*, Random House Business Books, 2001.

Chapter 6: Optimism

1 Collins, *Good to Great*.
2 Collins, *Good to Great*.
3 John F. Kennedy, speech at Rice University, 1962, https://er.jsc.nasa.gov/seh/ricetalk.htm.
4 Jana Nikitin and Alexandra M. Freund, "The Motivational Power of the Happy Face," *Brain Sciences* 9, 1 (2019): 6, https://www.ncbi.nlm.nih.gov/pmc/articles/PMC6356968/.
5 Nikitin and Freund, "The Motivational Power of the Happy Face."
6 Larry Stefan, *The Joy of Leadership*, self-published, 2016.

Chapter 7: Courage

1 Lao Tsu, *Tao Te Ching*, Vintage Books, 1972.
2 Thomas J. DeLong, *Flying without a Net*, Harvard Business School Press, 2011.
3 Linda Adams, "Learning a New Skill Is Easier Said Than Done," Gordon Training, n.d., https://www.gordontraining.com/free-workplace-articles/learning-a-new-skill-is-easier-said-than-done/.
4 Walter Isaacson, *Einstein: His Life and Universe*, Simon & Schuster, 2007.
5 Amos Tversky and Daniel Kahneman, "Advances in Prospect Theory: Cumulative Representation of Uncertainty," *Journal of Risk and Uncertainty* 5, 4 (1992): 297–323, https://www.jstor.org/stable/41755005.
6 Lyle Brenner, Yuval Rottenstreich, Sanjay Sood, and Baler Bilgin, "On the Psychology of Loss Aversion: Possession, Valence, and Reversals of the Endowment Effect," *Journal of Consumer Research* 34, 3 (October 2007): 369–76, https://www.jstor.org/stable/10.1086/518545.
7 *Encyclopaedia Britannica Online*, s.v. "Newton's Laws of Motion," accessed July 23, 2021, https://www.britannica.com/science/Newtons-laws-of-motion.
8 Kathleen K. Reardon, "Courage as a Skill," *Harvard Business Review*, January 2007, https://hbr.org/2007/01/courage-as-a-skill.
9 John McCain, "In Search of Courage," *Fast Company*, September 2004, https://www.fastcompany.com/50692/search-courage.

Chapter 8: Discipline

1 Walter Mischel, *The Marshmallow Test: Mastering Self-Control*, Little, Brown Spark, 2014.

2 Sam Goldstein, Key #9 in "The Power to Change Your Life," n.d., https://samgoldstein.com/resources/articles/general/the-power-to-change-your-life.aspx.

3 Mischel, *The Marshmallow Test*.

4 John Coleman, "Faced with Distraction, We Need Willpower," *Harvard Business Review*, February 22, 2012, https://hbr.org/2012/02/faced-with-distraction-we-need.

5 David Hamilton, *Social Cognition*, Taylor & Francis, 2004.

6 Discovery in Action, "Behavioural Change Is the Holy Grail of Leadership Development," Discovery in Action, n.d., https://discoveryinaction.com.au/behavioural-change-is-the-holy-grail-of-leadership-development/.

7 Megan Call, "Why Is Behavior Change So Hard?" *Accelerate*, February 14, 2020, https://accelerate.uofuhealth.utah.edu/explore/why-is-behavior-change-so-hard.

Conclusion

1 Helen Reddy, vocalist, "I Am Woman," by Ray Burton and Helen Reddy, produced by Jay Senter, Capitol Records, 1972.

INDEX

ABOUT THE AUTHORS

ALI GROVUE is a senior consultant at Ignite Management Services where she facilitates strategy and leadership development for individuals and teams within organizations across Canada. She is an expert in organizational strategy and leadership development, having earned a degree with honors in organizational behavior from the University of British Columbia and has also completed Leadership Coaching training at Harvard University. Ali has served in a range of leadership roles, including chief operating officer of a clean-tech company, executive director of a nonprofit association, and officer in the Royal Canadian Navy. She lives in Vancouver with her partner, Jamie.

MIKE WATSON is one of those individuals who consistently finds himself in "once in a lifetime" moments in sports and business. These experiences have put him in the company of phenomenal leaders that he has both coached and learned from. Mike believes that the well-being of employees is not only a business imperative but a moral obligation and that, with a defined plan of action, companies and their leaders can achieve great business results with inspired people who are on a journey to be the best versions of themselves. Mike is a master facilitator and strategic planner and has advised CEOs and boards across a range of industries. He has extensive advisory experience in the maritime and family enterprise spaces, has served as the VP of progressive, midsized financial firms, and is a past director of the Canadian Chamber of Commerce and the past chair of both the BC Chamber of Commerce and the North Vancouver Chamber of Commerce.

Are You a Resilient Leader?

T HE IGNITE MANAGEMENT SERVICES "Habits Assessment" will help you understand your own leadership style based on the six habits featured in this book and provide customized recommendations for how to improve your leadership. The assessment was developed in collaboration with industrial psychologists and clinical counselors and is based on hundreds of hours spent working with CEOs and senior leaders across multiple sectors.

Scan the QR code below to take the assessment.